MANIFESTING
FOR BEGINNERS

MANIFESTING
FOR BEGINNERS

A STEP-BY-STEP GUIDE TO ATTRACTING A LIFE YOU LOVE

VICTORIA JACKSON

ASTER✶

First published in Great Britain in 2022 by Aster, an imprint of
Octopus Publishing Group Ltd
Carmelite House
50 Victoria Embankment
London EC4Y 0DZ
www.octopusbooks.co.uk

An Hachette UK Company
www.hachette.co.uk

ISBN 978-1-78325-519-1

A CIP catalogue record for this book is available from the
British Library.

Printed and bound in China

10 9 8 7 6 5 4 3 2 1

Senior Commissioning Editor: Natalie Bradley
Art Director: Juliette Norsworthy
Editor: Sarah Kyle
Designer: Rosamund Saunders
Illustrator: Elise Conlin
Senior Production Controller: Emily Noto

Contents

Preface

If you had told me as a stressed, cynical, 20-something journalist that by the time I hit 30 I'd be surrounded by crystals, meditating each morning and spending my days teaching people how to use the power of their thoughts to shift their reality, I'd have scoffed.

Scrap that. I'd have scoffed and dropped the tiny violin I insisted on playing daily, as I eye-rolled so hard only the whites could be seen. You see, when you believe that life happens to you, rather than for you, it is hard to shift that negative, victim mentality many of us find ourselves experiencing on a day-to-day basis.

Life just happens and there is nothing we can do to control the outcome, right? Wrong.

On paper, my life was good. By the time I was 25, I had worked up the ranks to become the editor-in-chief of a men's fashion magazine. I travelled the world each year and was lucky enough to meet some amazing people on my journeys.

To those who followed me on social media, the highlights were all glitz, glam and another stamp in my passport.

Except that, away from the stress and late nights, I felt stuck in this energetic limbo of knowing that while I had so much to be grateful for, I craved more. Have you ever experienced the feeling of posting on Instagram and then sitting in guilt because you know what you've just shared is pretty far from reality?

I craved something more soul connected. Something that fulfilled me. Something that made me excited to wake up in the morning, rather than burying my head in paper towels as I cried in the ladies' room.

And just like that, right at the stage in life when I needed it most, I came across a book explaining the concept of the law of attraction and its partner in magic, manifestation.

My discovery of manifestation could have simply been a coincidence, or it could have been put in my path by a higher power to help me find the life I was meant to live. My hope is, by the time you finish the last page in this book, you'll believe the answer to be the latter.

As anyone with an all-or-nothing personality like mine does, I devoured every piece of knowledge I could about this unfamiliar concept. I listened to audiobooks as I drove to work, every plane journey would feature a new book, and I scoured the internet for real-life stories of manifestation working. I suddenly found myself in this new world of experts, studies and spiritual enlightenment.

I felt an affinity with the idea that there was a higher power guiding me on this path we call life. For you, it may be Source, God or even your spirit guides and ancestors; for me, it was the universe. I'd reached a point in life where I had no clue which way to turn next, and this was something I could

finally have faith in to steer me in the right direction.

If you are familiar with the phrase 'ask, believe, receive' – which is synonymous with manifestation – then you'll know we ask the universe for our desire, we believe it to already be ours and on its way to us, and we are open to receiving it however it may come into our lives.

I began with small experiments to see if my cynical outlook could be altered. Truth be told, I started small because I didn't understand how attracting something into your life through your thoughts could be possible. I was certainly open to believing a new reality, but I needed proof to build trust, just like we do with anything uncomfortable and new.

Armed with this knowledge, I asked the universe to show me a bright pink feather, and then I waited patiently for it to arrive. OK, patiently might be a lie. At this point, I could pretend I surrendered to the universe and didn't think about it again. In fact, that little pink feather consumed my thoughts.

'Oh, a feather on the ground! Has that white got an undertone of pink to it?'

'Big Bird from *Sesame Street*! When I asked for a pink feather, universe, did you hear yellow? Is this my manifestation?'

'Hang on, the sunset is pink! Did you think I said pink weather instead of pink feather, universe?'

Sure enough, two days later, an envelope came through the post, and stuck to the letter was a bright pink feather. Coincidence?

At first, I thought it could be. But as I continued to work on developing a more positive mindset and building trust that my thoughts could have more power than I believed, I began manifesting more and more into my life – be it a parking space, a friend texting after I thought about them, a free coffee as I sat in my favourite coffee shop, an ex-boyfriend getting back in touch to give me the closure I asked for, or even a lump sum of money from a lottery win or unexpected refund. In the space of three years, I had manifested close to £200,000 into my life and business.

And then the story takes us to the one manifestation that changed the trajectory of my life.

One Sunday evening, I sat in bed and asked the universe to help me find a way out of the career I was in. I closed my eyes and imagined what it would be like to work for myself, to build something of my own. I didn't know exactly what I was drawn to, but I imagined how it would feel to have the freedom to work anywhere in the world. To sit with my laptop and write. To share my experiences. To never have a cap on how much I could earn or be told I couldn't book time off for a holiday.

'The phrase "ask, believe, receive" is synonymous with manifestation'

The very next day, my magazine was closed down and I was made redundant. If ever there was a sign from the universe to make the leap, this was it.

And leap I did.

Which leads us to now, as I sit writing as a certified mindset coach, specializing in Neural Energetic Wiring and Neural Energetic Encoding, Hypnosis practitioner, an EFT (Emotional Freedom Technique) practitioner, community leader, number-one-charting podcast host, and founder of The Manifestation Collective, an online community guiding thousands of people across the world through shifting their reality using the power of their thoughts.

In all honesty, I feel like I'm a different person to the woman I described at the start of this preface. I continue to attract a life I truly love, and my aim through the pages of this book is to help you do the same.

INTRODUCTION

Manifestation may still feel like a new phenomenon to many, with social media propelling it to pop-culture status, but the ancient principles of the law of attraction have been discussed and utilized for centuries.

Manifesting and the law of attraction

In its simplest form, the law of attraction is the universal law stating that like attracts like. The more positive thoughts and intentions you put out into the world, the more positive energy you welcome back like a magnet. Similarly, the more negative your outlook, the more negative opportunities, people and situations you become aware of around you.

Manifestation, meanwhile, is the art of using your thoughts to create your reality and attract your specific desires. After all, the definition of 'to manifest' is to make something happen.

———

You and I have been manifesting since the day we were born. Perhaps not consciously, but we've been manifesting all the same. I can recall numerous times as a child when I thought I had magical powers, watching something I had imagined come to fruition yet again. Was I psychic? Was I a witch?! Or was I someone who truly manifested dresses worn over jeans as a 1990s trend?

When combined, the law of attraction and manifestation are powerful and life-changing tools – something we will be exploring throughout this book.

'Manifestation is the art of using your thoughts to create your reality and attract your specific desires'

The history of manifesting

When we consider the origins of manifestation, we learn that alternative teachings and abstract views on the power of our thoughts have been around for centuries.

The term 'law of attraction' was not referenced in literature until the 1870s, when Russian author and philosopher Helena Blavatsky spoke of the connection between spirits. However, the New Thought movement, which had begun to take shape in the early 19th century, as well as in religious teachings prior to that, often shared the belief that what we put out into the world would return to us.

In the 20th century, thinkers such as Napoleon Hill (who wrote *Think and Grow Rich*), Norman Vincent Peale (author of *The Power of Positive Thinking*) and Louise Hay (who penned *You Can Heal Your Life*) delved deeper into the spiritual ideology behind the law of attraction.

However, one of the most mainstream forays into the world of manifestation came from writer and television producer Rhonda Byrne, creator of *The Secret* – a documentary film and book now synonymous with the law of attraction. Heck, if something as alternative as *The Secret* is featured on Netflix, you know there is potential for a cult-like following.

This breakthrough into conventional media allowed a plethora of minds to suddenly open to an alternative and more positive way of thinking. And, just like that, the world began to hear stories of how household names were embracing the power of manifestation.

Talk show host and actress Oprah Winfrey has shared many stories of her manifestation wins, but none was so powerful as her part in the 1985 film adaptation of Alice Walker's book *The Color Purple*. After reading the book and being touched deeply by its story, Winfrey actively wished to land a part in a movie adaptation of it. One day she received a call from a casting agent asking her to audition for a film, which turned out to be *The Color Purple*. Months passed, and while the actress prayed and focused on surrendering to whatever the universe had in store, there was still no news. That was, until she fully released her grip on the outcome, whereupon she received a phone call from director Steven Spielberg offering her a part in the film.

The actor Jim Carrey has shared his story of writing a cheque to himself for $10 million in 1985 while he was an unknown name, still carving out a career in Hollywood. He dated the cheque ten years into the future and then carried it in his wallet for the next decade. Whether it was just sheer coincidence or the most amazing story of the universe's power, in 1995 – exactly ten years later – Carrey was offered a role in *Dumb and Dumber* with the payment of, you guessed it, $10 million.

You might be thinking, 'So, I can rub this hypothetical magic manifestation lamp and a genie will appear to grant me my biggest wishes?'

Yes and no. While the genie firmly belongs in *The Arabian Nights*, manifestation truly can turn your dreams into reality when consciously embraced.

However, if the idea of 'ask, believe, receive' were as simple as those three words, there would be no need for this book. Surely every human on earth would get every wish they ever desired, and we would be living in a state of continued abundance.

The reason this isn't a reality is that, generally, humans are still unaware of the true power of thought. Yes, millions worldwide have mastered the art of manifestation to attract love, happiness, wealth and healing health, but for most people it is still an unheard-of concept or is dismissed as nonsense.

The laws of the universe

To understand how manifestation works on a spiritual level, we first need to consider the laws of the universe. While the law of attraction is the shining star of this book, there are, in fact, a number of universal laws that cannot be seen but are, nonetheless, sewn into the fabric of everyday life.

According to the *law of oneness*, we are all as one within the universe, working together under an infinite power, whether that be a living creature, nature or energy. When you consider that plants create oxygen to keep humans alive, humans breathe out the carbon dioxide that plants live on, and our bodies aid lush growth when we are buried, you can see the law of oneness at play. We are all interconnected through the circle of divine oneness, meaning every choice you make has a ripple effect into the world.

The *law of compensation* focuses on the idea of receiving back what you put out into the world. The familiar phrase 'you reap what you sow' sums this up perfectly.

The *law of rhythm* is the universal reminder that everything passes and that life moves in cycles. Every season changes while time continues to move forward, moment by moment. This is a beautiful reminder to anyone who may be stuck in a challenging season right now.

When it comes to the *law of attraction*, it is said that we attract what we believe through the power of thought and energy – complemented by another universal law, the *law of vibration*. Although appearing to be still or solid matter, everything around us, including this book and your own body, is made up of energy vibrating at different speeds. The law of attraction dictates that the frequency at which we are vibrating magnetizes the same frequency back to us.

Radio High Vibe

When we are emitting a particular frequency, we tune into similar frequencies – just like when we are tuning into a favourite radio station. Let's call this Radio High Vibe. And how do we control the frequency of vibration? Through the power of our thoughts.

When we are experiencing high-vibrational thoughts of gratitude, joy, excitement and optimism, the energy of our bodies increases. In contrast, when we are in a lower state of mind, experiencing thoughts of anger, resentment, frustration, guilt or unworthiness, we vibrate at a lower frequency.

Have you ever noticed how, when you are in a great mood, other people of a similar temperament are attracted to you, things seem to flow, and little moments, like finding a parking space or discovering money in an old handbag, seem to make the day a little easier? This is a perfect example of being tuned in to Radio High Vibe.

At the opposite end of the scale, when you have woken up on the wrong side of the bed, spilled mouthwash all over the bathroom, hit your elbow on the corner of a drawer and started the day with a negative mindset, life feels that much harder. When we are feeling in a low state of mind, our bodies are vibrating at a lower frequency, and we attract people and situations that are in harmony with the same vibration.

How do we alter our emotions to change the vibration of our bodies? Through the power of our thoughts.

Nevertheless, no amount of positive thoughts can truly shift your vibrational frequency if the paradigm – the set of habits and information that have programmed your subconscious mind – isn't altered first. This explains why not everyone has the power to manifest their dreams just by asking the universe and thinking positive thoughts. First, you have to shift those limiting beliefs that have been ingrained into your subconscious mind.

We can ask, but if we do not believe, how can we receive?

The good news is that throughout the following chapters there will be tools and tips aplenty to help you start unlocking the power of your subconscious mind, enabling you to harness the powers of conscious manifesting.

Take this book, for example. I truly believe I manifested the opportunity to write these very pages. First, as a seven-year-old, I informed my parents that I intended to be a 'bookie' when I grew up. (By that, of course, I meant I wanted to write books. I was puzzled as to why my parents were laughing at my saying I wanted to manage sporting bets for a living.) And second, several years ago, I recorded on social media that one day – with the help of the universe – I would sign a publishing contract.

I spoke this book into existence. I didn't know the how or the when, but I knew that I could take action to meet the universe halfway. By sharing my writing online, as well as by doing the mindset work I needed to do in order to believe I was worthy of such a project, and by stepping into the high-vibrational energy of excitement over the possibility of seeing my name on bookshelves across the world, I could attract suitable opportunities to make it happen.

To manifest is to think about what you truly want from life, to ask the higher power of the universe to help deliver this intention, and to look for ways in which it could arrive through harmonious opportunities, people, places and actions. It is to believe your manifestation to already be yours, just waiting to be drawn in when you are at the right energetic match to attract it to you.

STEP
1

Visualize your future self

What is your soul calling you to do? That one
question can either evoke a heartfelt response
or cause people to stare blankly as they wonder
whether they actually *have* a soul and, if so,
why it isn't speaking to them. So, before we
step into discovering how to truly embrace the
magic of manifestation, I want to discuss the
power of current you vs. future you.

Living in alignment

The process of stepping into your highest self
– the version of you that embodies your fullest,
most joyous potential – is not an easy feat. But,
rewarding? Rewarding it most certainly is.

Let me caveat this by saying the current version
of you is exactly who you are meant to be at this
moment in time. The work I do, including writing this
book, is never designed to make you examine what is
wrong, but rather to create space for you to decide
what areas of life you would like to amplify – where
you want to increase the vibration and switch things
up in the most positive of ways.

You deserve to live a life you wake up feeling
excited about – a life of alignment. The word
'alignment' crops up frequently in this book, as
it has become synonymous with manifestation.
To live in alignment is to feel a sense of harmony
throughout all areas of your life, with a unity
between your soul goals (see pages 29–33) and
your actions. Feeling anxious, unsettled, tired
or irritable, or just having a gut feeling that
something is 'off', is a sign that you are spiritually
out of alignment.

> *'You deserve to live*
> *a life you wake up feeling*
> *excited about'*

Embracing change

When we talk about creating a life we love, this isn't about toxic positivity. The last thing I want us to create is a false sense of happiness, where we jump out of bed into a sea of roses and skip to work to the sound of birds singing. Instead, it is about shifting our thoughts to welcome a new sense of possibility into our lives, and turning our daydreams into tangible moments in time.

You see, the trouble with life for many of us is that we are living on repeat, feeling like we are unable to stop the hamster wheel. We're unable to see what areas of our lives need work and where our true happiness really comes from, because our minds are taken up with the daily grind.

The reason this resonates so strongly with me is that I lived in this energy for close to a decade. I remember one time in particular driving to work, cursing the hours I was wasting sitting in traffic on my daily commute, not looking forward to the day, worrying about deadlines, annoyed at myself for pressing snooze instead of getting up earlier, and thinking…is this it? Is this my life now?

It felt like the negative thoughts were spiralling out of control, and like my body was vibrating at such a low frequency that I was unable even to spot the great things in life, never mind appreciate them. What was worse, I made no effort to change.

The truth is, many of us are hesitant to stop living a 'photocopied' life, repetitive and predictable, because, even if it doesn't necessarily fulfil us, there is an element of comfort there. And if there's one thing the mind likes, it's being within its comfort zone.

Constantly looking to reserve its energy, the mind will try to return to default mode as soon as possible. It is built to streamline everything – including both good and bad habits – and puts them on automatic repeat within the limbic system (the part of the brain that processes your memories, emotions, habits and behaviours) so that it doesn't have to work as hard.

After all, the mind is processing millions of pieces of information every single minute, filtering each piece to decide what is or isn't useful and whether there is a need to activate fight-or-flight mode. Its sole job is to keep us safe.

Which is why making positive changes can feel so tough at the beginning. You're forcing the mind to alter, and its first instinct is to resist. However, the great thing about the subconscious mind is that it can be reprogrammed with new beliefs and habits.

What's more, there is no better time than now to embrace a change in mind, body and soul.

Never before has our generation had to face such uncertain situations, from climate change to global lockdowns, economic crises and unstable job markets. It's no wonder the thought of stepping out of its comfort zone is too much for the mind to comprehend.

But we are also a generation that has more choice than ever. More accessibility. More opportunity. The beauty of the uncertainty we

are experiencing is the possibility that lies within it. However, to truly lean in to the energy of possibility, we have to be both self-aware and present.

Ask yourself this – are you living a life that is manipulated and moulded by society, including friends and family, into the version of you they envision?

It is so easy to become someone other people want us to be. Perhaps you studied a subject purely because your parents expected you to do so. Or maybe you settled into an unfulfilling relationship because the thought of being the only single person in a friendship group scared you. Perhaps you are currently in a toxic work environment and you dream about one day running your own business, but the thought of what others will say causes so much resistance, you can't seem to put one foot in front of the other.

Without consciously knowing, you have manifested these situations into your life through thoughts, behaviours and actions.

The good news? With the teachings of manifestation, you can now consciously attract an alternative reality.

Eight-line exercise

This is one of the first tools you can use to understand which areas of your life you would like to positively amplify. It involves drawing eight lines, with the numbers 1 to 10 marked evenly along each one. Each line represents one of the following categories for you to think about:

Family + friends: Consider how satisfied you are with the relationships in your life: your family, friendships and communication with others.

Love: Consider how you feel about the love you have in your life, both romantic and non-romantic. Have you met your soulmate yet? Are you sexually satisfied? Does communication need work? Do you crave more adventure?

Health + wellbeing: Consider the way you feel about both your physical and mental wellbeing. Think about how much you move throughout the day, your moods, how much fresh air you get, how much energy you have on an average day, and how much sleep you get.

Along each line, mark how fulfilled you feel – number one being the least happy, number ten being the most fulfilled you could be.
You should now have a clear representation of which areas of your life have scored highly and which areas need work. Don't worry if most areas are low on the scale – acknowledgment is the first step toward change.

1   2   3   4   5

Self-development: Consider whether you prioritize self-development, whether you want more time to read and to educate yourself on particular subjects, whether you'd like coaching in a certain area of life, and how satisfied you are with your level of personal growth right now.

Career: Consider whether you are in a job that makes you happy, whether working for yourself could one day be a reality, what tasks in your career bring you the most fulfilment, and how the scales tip in terms of the elusive work–life balance.

Money: Consider your income, your outgoings, what the money you attract allows you to do and how you feel about your current financial situation.

Environment: Consider your surroundings: where you live, your home, your neighbours and whoever shares your space.

Spirituality or religion: Consider whether you feel as aligned to your religion as you'd like to be or, if you are spiritual, whether you have time to work further on this. Think about your beliefs, what your spiritual practices are and which practices you draw the most happiness from.

6　　7　　8　　9　　10

Identify your soul goals

Let me take this moment to introduce soul goals. Rather than high-achieving goals that you strive toward purely for external success – for example, reaching the top of the career ladder for that six-figure salary, or attaining a designer bag not because you love it but because of the image it portrays – soul goals are goals that feed your soul.

Soul goals don't have monetary value or materialistic significance. They are not fuelled by our egos, telling us we have to achieve something so society can reaffirm we are on the right path for a person of our age.

You see, the trouble with setting goals is that we often set them with the intention of finding happiness at the end of the rainbow. But there is no end, and, at any rate, the happiness we feel is fleeting, which leads us to move the goalposts again and again. We spend our lives chasing the next big thing, the next big thrill. But when it doesn't feed the soul, that next thing is only momentary.

I set the goal of becoming the editor of a magazine before I was 30, and by the age of 25 I'd reached that point. At first, I felt like I'd reached the pinnacle career-wise. But it didn't last. As the years passed, my soul felt like it was sitting there, empty.

It wasn't until the universe led me to building this business and teaching about manifestation that my soul really lit up. Bursting into a ball of flames is actually a more apt description of it.

A soul goal doesn't need to be your life's purpose. It doesn't need to be a complete 180-degree career change. It doesn't need to be a life upheaval. It can be simply feeding your need to travel and explore the world. It can be wanting to live a harmonious, balanced life filled with music, laughter and happiness. It can be working for someone else, while creating the most amazing joy-filled home to return to after work or school. It can be teaching other people a skill you've developed and grown.

Ask yourself this – am I wanting to attract this into my life for internal happiness or external validation? One thing I often find myself asking coaching clients is, if you couldn't share this on social media, would you still want it? In today's society, plagued by the need to be seen, liked and validated by strangers online, this is a question we have to continually ask ourselves.

'If you couldn't share this on social media, would you still want it?'

How to gain clarity on your soul goals

Gaining clarity on how you would like your life to look and feel can be challenging if you are new to personal development work. Here are three ways to lean in to the energy of exploration.

Take responsibility

Clarity isn't going to arrive on your doorstep – you need to take responsibility for your decisions. When it comes to personal development, self-awareness will be your best friend. On the next page, you will find a series of journal prompts designed to help you unlock thoughts, recognize resistance and notice dreams that might have been buried under the surface.

Explore

Don't be afraid to explore and experiment. Clarity doesn't come from waiting for the right thing to land in your lap, so experiment with different goals until you find something that aligns. Don't be afraid of trial and error. Your tastes and preferences will change over time, so be kind to yourself if what you wanted a year ago isn't what you want now. The universe will never let you fail; it will only help you learn a lesson or embrace a blessing.

Notice who or what is stopping you

Do you spend time with people who are not in alignment with the future you? Do you numb yourself with food, drink or other addictions? Do you distract yourself with Netflix, YouTube or video games?

There are certain things that we do in life that stop us from being able to get real clarity over what we truly want. However uncomfortable it might feel at first, by turning the dial down on these distractions we are able to tune in more clearly to our internal guide.

Nobody knows what you want for your future self other than you. Remember that.

Amplify your manifesting magic with... these journal prompts

Unearth those soul goals by taking a journal, finding a peaceful moment, getting comfortable and then putting pen to paper to answer whichever prompts shown here are calling to you.

- Are you happy with your career/business right now? If not, why not?

- What would you change if there were no limitations or restrictions?

- How do you dream about spending your days?

- What would you do with your career/business if you were guaranteed success?

- What small changes could you make today to help your job/business be a happier place?

- How does competition make you feel?

- What are you grateful for in your career right now?

- When are you at your most productive?

- What values do you look for in a partner?

- Who are the people that mean the most to you and how can you be intentional about spending time with these people?

- What limiting beliefs come up for you when you think about your soulmate?

- How can you rewrite these stories?

- Who do you need to forgive?

- How can you love yourself more?

- When are you at your happiest in a relationship?

- Describe your dream date.

- How could you welcome more love into your life?

- Write down your ideal vision of your life. What are three ways you can take action toward this vision?

- What do you think about before you go to sleep?

- How have you made yourself proud recently?

- What are five things you can do less often?

- What do you miss?

- When do you feel most confident?

- If today was your last day, what would you do?

- If you could be anywhere in the world right now, where would you be?

- What do you want the view out of your window to look like?

- What positive changes can you make to your home environment?

- What are you most grateful for in your home right now?

- What is causing you stress at home, and what can be done to work toward solving this?

- What would make your home more relaxing?

- Without limitations or restrictions, describe in detail what your dream home would be like.

- What is no longer serving you at home?

- Do you feel truly at home?

- What beliefs did your parents have about money?

- What is your dream income each month?

- Describe your relationship with money in five words.

- How do you want to feel about money?

- Do you tie your self-worth to how much money you make?

- Do you judge others on how much money they have?

- What is your biggest fear around money?

- If you had unlimited money, what would change?

- List all of the different ways in which money could flow to you.

STEP
2

Set your intentions

You may be familiar with the phrase 'intention setting'. Along with 'mindfulness' and 'abundance', intention setting has become a trend within New Age spirituality, but in its basic form, it denotes creating a life with direction.

Soul goals vs. intentions

In this chapter we discuss the art of setting an intention, moving away from the spiritual aspect and toward the strategy behind it.

Let's first consider the difference between intentions and soul goals (see pages 29–33). Imagine you are going on a road trip for a moment. The destination is your soul goal, while intention setting is the map that helps you arrive with focus and speed. Setting intentions allows us to reach our soul goals with purpose, rather than driving without direction and hoping for the best. For example, one of your soul goals could be to be truly happy in your career, while the intention you set could be attracting a new role, manifesting a promotion or calling in a new team to surround yourself with.

Think of the soul goal as the place you'd like to end up and the intention as the sat nav.

An intention allows us to inform the universe of what it is we are wanting to call into our lives. While the work we have done as part of the previous chapter has allowed us to look inward in a general capacity, now is the time to reflect on what specific things we would like to manifest.

Throughout this book, our aim is to return to our natural flow state of happiness and move away from the need for external validation, but I don't want to discredit the desire for material items. Living a human existence means the want and need for tangible things is very much a reality and should therefore be honoured.

Making connections

Modern manifestation can be defined as a blend of spirituality, soul and science. It is about understanding the basics of neuroscience and how setting a positive intention changes your thought pattern, which in turn changes your behaviour, thus altering the actions you take on a daily basis toward building a fulfilled and aligned life.

You see, when you set an intention, your reticular activating system (or reticular formation) – a sophisticated system of nerves sitting at the end of your brainstem – chooses what to focus on and filters out other pieces of information that are not relevant to the goal at hand. Which is why, for example, when you choose to buy a new car, you suddenly feel like the roads are overrun with your chosen model. Or why you can pick out your own name being shouted in a screaming crowd of people.

———

However, if you do not feel aligned to your intention in mind, body and soul, there will always be some form of energy barrier. In her 2019 book *The Source: Open Your Mind. Change Your Life*, neuroscientist and former psychiatric doctor Tara Swart speaks of the meeting point of our intention. When you are fully aligned to your goal and understand your why, then your intuition, deepest emotions and rational thinking work in harmony, rather than in conflict. As Swart explains, it is almost impossible to reach your goals when you are out of kilter in these three dimensions. As humans, we think of the head, heart and gut as separate entities – how many times have you played a hypothetical game of tug of war between your heart and head when making a difficult decision? In fact, scientists continue to discover more and more about the connection between our thoughts, our emotions and our physical being.

The question of specificity

When we look at our goals, the one question that can often cause confusion is: how specific should we be?

Spiritual gurus and guides to the law of attraction will often tell us that the universe knows best and will deliver to us what is most needed. While this is certainly true (and will be discussed in a moment), how does the universe know what to bring into your life if your intention is vague?

There is a fine line between calling in what you would like to manifest and being fluid enough to release the desire and understand that it will arrive exactly how and when it was meant to – even if it doesn't look like what you initially envisioned.

The thing to remember is that the universe has only three possible responses to your manifestation:

Yes.

Be patient.

I have something even better suited.

However, where specificity comes into play is in giving the universe at least a hint of what you'd like to attract. For example, you could set the intention to attract more money into your life, and the very next day find a penny on the street. That penny lying on the cold hard ground signifies more money. But you and I both know that when you set the intention to attract more money, it probably wasn't a penny you were imagining. In this instance, get specific on the amount of money you would like to manifest, and release your grip on the how and when it will arrive.

—

As someone who has manifested various lump sums of money into her life over the last five years, I have found that the how and when are often unexpected. Refunds from the bank, a loan suddenly repaid, projects with a much higher budget than expected, winning competitions – the way I have magnetized money has become a source of amusement among my friends and family.

Perhaps you would like a promotion at work, or a new car? Would you like to attract more money into your savings account, or maybe the opportunity to have your business featured in the press? Could there be an intention to meet your soulmate or finally find your dream beach house?

Take the soulmate, for example. The idea is to focus on how that person would make you feel, how you would spend time together, whether they'd be funny, kind-hearted, or a great communicator. Really consider the characteristics of a person who would set your soul (and pants) on fire.

The nitty-gritty of physical appearance, how you are going to meet them and the timescale for when it will happen aren't any of your business – you have to relinquish that control to the universe. Otherwise, you could have your heart set on someone with dark hair and miss your blond soulmate standing there under the flashing lights of the universe.

Maybe you've been searching for months for that dream house and your list of essentials is as long as your arm. It must have

> ‘*We have to relinquish that control to the universe*’

four bedrooms, must have a large kitchen, must have garden space. But what if a house in an ideal location appeared, under budget, except with three bedrooms and a large attic? Could this be the universe pointing its wand in the direction of a potential you might not have seen if your filters had been on?

Perhaps you're looking for a dream job, but you're not sure what it is you want next in your career. Perfect: you can sit and ask yourself how you want to feel at work, what your desired salary is, whether you want to work in a team or solo, how you would spend your days, whether you want to work from home or in an office environment – there are so many ways you can describe your ideal job, without focusing a particular job title.

Can you see how there is a need to outline what it is you are wanting to manifest so both you and the universe have clarity, without becoming bogged down in the small details? Otherwise, there is a risk that you shut off all of the different ways in which your desire could be delivered.

Your cosmic shopping list

This style of manifesting – creating a list of specifics – has been dubbed writing a 'cosmic shopping list'. It's like writing a list before you head to the store, except instead of things to fill the kitchen cabinets, you're choosing what you'd like to fill your life with.

Keep your list somewhere safe so that when the universe delivers what could potentially be your desire, you can refer to your list to see if your vision aligns with what the universe has sent. In situations where the universe brings to you something amazing but not quite right, this provides the perfect opportunity to re-evaluate your manifestation.

———

Every situation, whether it be a relationship that didn't work as planned, or a house sale that fell through, or perhaps a job interview that didn't go the way you envisioned, provides a chance to fine-tune your list of specifics.

When we look at specificity and the setting of intentions, a fundamental part of cementing what it is we'd like the universe to help us attract is understanding our 'why'.

When we feel out of alignment in life, it can often be down to losing sight of our 'why' – why we want to live a particular lifestyle, build a business, or make a positive change to our mindset.

Connecting to the reason we want to manifest something into our lives elicits an emotional response, and in turn it helps us lean into the energy of the possibility of it happening. And what happens when our energy matches that of what we want to attract? It is magnetized to us.

For example, if you want to manifest the opportunity to leave your 9–5 job and build your own business, knowing your why is imperative. Is it because you'd like to help people? Do you wish to make sure your children never have to want for anything? Is it because you'd like to make a social impact?

'Real shifts will occur when you focus internally rather than seeking external validation'

Is it because you want to make someone feel calm and at peace every time they use your product? Or would you like them to feel confident and as though they can take on the world after using your service?

Take a moment to think about why you want to manifest the things you do. It doesn't need to be a life-changing, Nobel Peace Prize-inspired why, but real shifts will occur when you focus internally rather than seeking external validation.

Fear of vocalizing your dreams

Perhaps right now you are experiencing a familiar feeling. It's almost like your dreams are on the tip of your tongue, but you swallow them again. Fear of vocalizing our dreams presents a very valid challenge.

Although fear is discussed at various points throughout this book, for now we can acknowledge that fear is a natural, powerful and primitive human emotion. It alerts you to the presence of danger or the threat of harm, whether that danger is physical or psychological. Fear in the primal sense is absolutely real – your body goes into fight-or-flight mode to protect you from being eaten by tigers or run over by a bus.

But the fear of judgment online, or from colleagues, family or friends, is different. It is often a fear of not wanting to process the emotions that can come from putting yourself out of your comfort zone and into the path of potential 'failure'.

Perhaps you're pre-empting the possible feeling of shame, of embarrassment, of guilt, even, that might stem from vocalizing dreams that don't then automatically come to fruition.

Your subconscious mind has been programmed from an early age to fear judgment and failure – most frustratingly, from external sources, such as your environment, upbringing and the media. What you should fear is what life will be like if you don't follow your true calling or natural instincts.

If being judged by others occupies your thoughts, consider this. Whether you follow your passions or not, there will always be someone with an opinion on how you live your life. The question is, would you rather get to the end of your life knowing that you stayed small to appease someone else, or would you like to live life to the fullest?

When people have a negative opinion or make a quick judgment, it is often because something in the situation is shining a mirror on their own fears, reflecting back a deep-rooted block in their own subconscious. It is not about you.

Amplify your manifesting magic with… a New Moon intention-setting ritual

Working with the energy of the moon is incredibly powerful, especially when it comes to setting your intentions with the universe.

The start of each lunar cycle, when the moon is in its first lunar phase, is the perfect chance to set new intentions for the month ahead and press the reset button on any stagnant energy you may have been experiencing. Despite the disc of the moon being in its darkest transition visible here on earth, this is a timely reminder that there is new possibility even in the darkest of times.

Integrating a regular New Moon ritual into your spiritual self-care routine allows you to consciously connect to the universe. You can recalibrate your energy during what is regarded as an incredibly potent time for goal setting and self-reflection.

Here are six ways in which you can embrace the New Moon energy (which comes around every 28–30 days) with a simple intention-setting ceremony.

Create space

A cluttered environment can often equate to a cluttered mind, so before you begin your New Moon ritual, create space within your home where you are able to sit in peace and comfort. This can be as simple as clearing space in your bedroom, drawing the curtains and lighting a candle, (ginger, sandalwood and orange are all powerful scents to use while taking part in any form of manifesting ritual, as they evoke the energy of love, empowerment and abundance).

Alternatively, you can create a simple spiritual self-care corner in the room of your choice, using a beanbag, floor cushions, plants and candles, plus a small table to act as a platform for any crystals you may have.

When you take the time to make space for your rituals and routines – especially in a busy household – it acts as a reminder that your mental, physical and spiritual health is just as important as everyone else's.

Cleanse

Once you have created space within the home, purify the area of any remaining negative energy by cleansing it. Traditionally, burning white sage (better known as smoke cleansing) has been used to disperse stagnant energy within a space or around objects.

Unfortunately, as a result of large retail companies selling increased quantities and the mainstream media now publicizing its powerful qualities, white sage is being over-harvested and is at risk of becoming endangered – often with no regard for the Native American customs from which white sage smoke cleansing originates.

There are, however, responsible smoke-cleansing alternatives, including burning cedar, pine or dried and bundled lavender. Incense is also an effective substitute, as is physically moving through the space with a selenite wand to disperse unwanted energy.

Focus on your breathing

The hustle of daily life can leave us feeling disconnected, which is why taking a few moments to focus on your breathing is an essential piece of your spiritual self-care jigsaw. Close your eyes and place your hand on your heart. Feel the rhythmic beat as you take four deep breaths in through your nose and out through your mouth. Drop your shoulders and imagine yourself sinking into the ground where you sit. From each breath, feel yourself become more and more grounded, connecting not only to the universe but to your own body. Begin to move your fingers and toes and welcome a flow of new energy.

Write your intentions for the month ahead

Before you let your pen touch the paper, sit and consider what you would like to call in for the month ahead. These three journal prompts could help unearth ideas:

• What goals would you like to work toward?

• What habits would you like to implement into your daily routine?

• What positive changes would you like to make during the next 30 days?

Take time to self-reflect and consider what you would like to draw in to your life. For example, do you wish to connect more to nature and take a daily walk? Perhaps you want to work on strengthening your friendships by speaking to three friends on the phone rather than exchanging text messages. Do you want to welcome in more opportunities for your business? Maybe your intention is to set aside some time to explore potential collaborations.

Here are a few examples of intentions you could write:

Under the energy of the New Moon, I call in the motivation to walk outside three times a week, during which I will reconnect with nature and raise my vibrations.

Under the energy of the New Moon, I call in more love and positive energy to my friendship circle, with the opportunity this month to spend quality time together.

Under the energy of the New Moon, I call in newly aligned opportunities for my business that will help me reach my financial goal of XYZ.

How many intentions should you set under the New Moon ritual? One to three is often the sweet spot between the intentions feeling achievable and feeling overwhelming. If you set the metaphorical bar too high, you could find yourself feeling you're 'back to square one' if you don't have 30 days of perfection. You are never back to square one, you are simply returning to the same spot on the path from which you took a slight detour. You are still closer to your goals than you were when you began your journey.

Seal your intentions

Hold the piece of paper containing your intentions, close your eyes and take a moment to visualize them coming to fruition. What do you see around you at the point of knowing your desires have been delivered for the month? What do you hear or say? How do you feel? Excited? Relieved? Happy? Lean in to that magnetic energy you feel within your body for a few moments and understand that this, right here, is the key to manifestation – stepping in to the feelings and emotions that you would feel if your month had gone exactly as planned.

Open your eyes and fold the piece of paper toward you to seal in this magnetic energy. Place it somewhere close to where you sleep – perhaps under your pillow or in your bedside drawer.

Take a detox bath

Finally, as part of your New Moon intention-setting ritual, run a warm bath and use Epsom salts to detoxify and cleanse ahead of the next lunar phase.

Be sure to drink water as you bathe to keep hydrated. Create ambience by leaving your phone in another room, lighting your favourite candles, placing crystals around the bath and creating a neck support with towels.

STEP
3

Connect with the universe

There are many ways in which we can communicate with the universe, and the beauty of it is that it can happen in any way you feel drawn to. In our day-to-day lives we all have our preferred styles of communication, and the same can be said for spiritual connection and energetic exchange. But first we need to allow ourselves space to connect to a higher source.

Connecting by disconnecting

With society becoming saturated with content, opinions and noise, it is no wonder that forming a connection to the universe and, more importantly, own inner guidance system, has become increasingly challenging. Perhaps it's time to locate the mute button for a moment?

Among the biggest saboteurs of our spiritual journey are social media, the internet and our phones. Not only are we in an era where our own desires are drowned out by what other people may have or may want, but also our attention spans are becoming worryingly short – so short that the idea of spending ten minutes meditating away from a phone can send some people into a cold sweat.

'Nothing but our own internal compass can indicate what we want to experience'

How is modern technology stopping us from connecting to the universe?

When we find ourselves constantly comparing our lives with those of others, it can block out what we truly want. We start to work toward goals that other people want or expect from us. We listen to everyone else but ourselves, when in fact nothing but our own internal compass can indicate what we want to experience.

So-called 'comparisonitis', the compulsion to compare your accomplishments with another's, is a very real issue in today's modern world. We know that social media provides a filtered view of reality, yet we struggle to resist measuring our own experiences against it, which is unfair.

———

Let's consider for a moment how often we block communication from the universe simply because we are heads down, fingers typing, completely and utterly fixated on emails and notifications.

Imagine if the universe was a friend or loved one – can you envisage the strain they'd feel if they kept trying to speak to you and you were constantly occupied with your phone? Or if they wanted to share a surprise and tried to steer you in the direction

of it, but you ignored all the signs because you were checking Instagram?

How many of us automatically grab our phones first thing in the morning, before we've even had time to let our eyes adjust to the natural light in the room? It becomes a habitual response to the start of the day, and we allow the (often negative) energy of the world to filter through before we're able to decide how we would like our days to look.

Instead of instantly reaching for your phone to turn your alarm off each morning, why not purchase an alarm clock and move your phone away from the bed? This creates a pattern interrupt, a technique used to change a particular behaviour – in this case, reaching for your phone as soon as you wake up – by forcing you to change your natural thought pattern.

Ways to connect to the universe

Think of this as a spiritual mix of ways to connect to the universe. Dip in and out of what you are feeling energetically pulled to do and, most importantly, enjoy the process.

Create a vision board

Building a visual representation of your dreams and goals is an incredibly effective way of gaining clarity on what you would like to manifest.

There are a number of ways you can do this, the first being the good old-fashioned route of cutting images and words out of magazines to make a vision board. A great tip is to buy a mixture of different magazines, from travel to fashion to wellness and beyond. This will give you a wide spectrum of ideas and images. (You can also create a digital version by saving images from websites such as Pinterest and Google, and keep it as a screensaver on your phone or your desktop background.)

While there may be material things you want to manifest into your life, the most important element of a vision board is for it to represent how you want to feel. For this reason, don't be afraid

to use more abstract visuals if they represent your future. The images and words you choose do not have to make sense to anyone but you, as long as they evoke a high-vibrating energy, such as excitement, optimism and happiness, when you look at them.

Do not overthink this process; there may be no obvious rhyme or reason to the visuals you find yourself drawn to, but trust that intrinsically you are being guided toward what it is you are looking for – whether that be consciously or subconsciously.

Once you have ripped out images and words that you feel connected to, lay everything out in front of you and see what you can eliminate and what you'd like to keep. Then grab some glue and a large piece of cardboard and start sticking.

Place your board somewhere you can see it daily and spend a few moments connecting to your manifestations. Let yourself lean in to the energy of how you will feel when these images have become your reality – because here is your reminder that it absolutely can be if you so choose.

Tip
One of the most powerful things you can do when looking at your vision board is smile, because your vibrations will naturally start to increase. Forcing a smile can trick the brain into thinking humour has happened, which then kickstarts neurotransmitters such as dopamine, serotonin and endorphins to boost your happiness levels.

Riff with a friend

To riff is to improvise aloud, like jazz musicians do, so what better way to speak your manifestations to the universe than sitting with a like-minded friend and creating a back-and-forth dialogue as if your desires have already become a reality. Tell your friend about the amazing (imaginary) date you've just come back from. Listen to them describe how their (also imaginary) business is growing. Alongside a stellar playlist, riffing with a friend is the ultimate way to spend a high-vibe road trip.

Tip
Riffing doesn't always have to include another person – one of my favourite ways to connect to the universe is to riff on my desires as I am driving, speaking them into existence. Let's describe it as making a spiritual call in the car.

Script your ideal day

Scripting is a manifestation technique where you sit and journal as if your manifestation has already materialized. By writing in the present tense as if your desires have already come to fruition, you are able to really embrace the energy of what it will feel like when it becomes a reality.

———

With this technique, you don't have to focus on one particular manifestation; you can also look at the wider picture of how you would like your life to take shape. It can be a great way of gaining clarity on how you'd like your day, week, month or even year to look. Think about it from the second you wake up – what time is it, how does the bedroom look, what does the bed feel like, what can you hear? Let yourself write without limitation and in as much detail as possible.

Tip

Here are ten scripting prompts to help you envision your ideal day:
- What time do you wake up?
- Is anyone lying next to you?
- What is your morning routine?
- What do you do for a living?
- How does the day look to you?
- What is your self-care routine?
- Do you have any spiritual routines such as meditation?
- How does your body feel?
- What does your ideal evening include?
- How do you feel just before you close your eyes to sleep?

Visualization

Put simply, visualization is the act of daydreaming, creating a movie within your mind to simulate what you would like your dream life to represent. It is where your thoughts, goals and ideas are represented by the millions upon millions of visual memories the subconscious mind has filtered and filed away over the years.

Just as the mind cannot differentiate between when you are genuinely smiling and when you are just going through the motions, it also can't tell whether a visualization is a reality or is imagined. This is why athletes will often use visualization techniques as part of their training, creating a movie in their mind of winning, of crossing the finish line, of landing the shot that takes them into the lead. It creates behavioural patterns and actions to help you align to your manifestations and creates the same output of high-vibrational energy.

Of course, this doesn't happen overnight. We don't daydream at our desks and then suddenly appear on the front cover of Forbes magazine. But regular moments of visualization, regardless of whether they are daily, weekly or even monthly, will help you become clear on what you would like to attract into your life and will make inspired action easier.

> *'Athletes will often use visualization techniques as part of their training'*

How to visualize

· Find somewhere quiet and comfortable to sit or lie down with your eyes closed.

· Take four deep breaths in through your nose and out through your mouth, feeling yourself sink into the ground beneath you as you connect to the universe.

· In your mind's eye, create a mental image – either static like a photo or fluid like a movie – of your desired manifestation. Imagine the finer details and focus on what emotions you are experiencing, what you can hear, and what you can smell, taste, touch. What do you look like as your highest self? What are you wearing? Notice everything around you in this visualization and begin to make the image brighter and more in focus.

· Amplify the positive feelings you have when you think of this visualization becoming your reality, and notice how your energy shifts – this can come in the form of tingling in your fingers, your breathing rate changing, a smile forming or even the urge to move your body.

· Remain in this energetic state for as long as you feel comfortable. Once you feel yourself begin to stir, bring your awareness back to your surroundings, open your eyes and trust in the power of possibility.

• There are various ways in which the mind receives information and stores it as a memory. It can be visual (through sight), olfactory (through smell), auditory (through sound), gustatory (through taste), tactile (through touch) or kinaesthetic (through feeling). However, visualization isn't always a straightforward process for some people. For example, it may prove challenging for you to visually create in your mind a movie of sitting on a beach and watching the waves roll in; however, a particular scent might evoke certain emotions and associations within the olfactory memory of being at the beach. Or maybe you'll find you can imagine a conversation and remember the sound of someone's voice through auditory memory, but you're unable to picture the person's face.

• This is why I refer to the technique as a pick 'n' mix situation. If one manifestation technique doesn't work for you, you can try something else that is better suited.

Tip
During your visualization, if you notice that you are seeing yourself in the image (disassociated), rather than being in the image looking through your own eyes (associated), visualize moving into your body. Do the emotions feel stronger? If you feel less connected, visualize moving out of your body and continue watching in third person.

Acting as if

Acting 'as if' is a technique primarily used in Cognitive Behavioural Therapy (CBT), which believes that changing our behaviour can change our thoughts. Similarly, acting as if our desired outcome is already a reality can change our thoughts so they become more aligned with our vision.

By altering your external circumstances and embracing more of an outside-in approach, you are able to change your habits, thoughts, behaviours and, ultimately, actions.

When I began my business, acting as if I was already a successful coach and community leader meant that I was able to build strong-enough foundations for the business to grow from. Before I even signed my first coaching client, I acted as if I had a diary full of calls and would schedule time to coach in my diary. I built an online portal for my future clients to store all of their notes from our calls. I created classes I wanted to teach them and recorded meditations I wanted them to listen to.

It was these external actions that led to the change in my mindset that helped me believe it was possible for me to run a successful business. Each day that I acted 'as if', the limiting beliefs I had were becoming more and more diluted, and my neural pathways were being remoulded to the shape of 'It *is* possible, because I am already doing it'.

Tip
Acting 'as if' has gained a questionable reputation online due to the idea that you have to spend money to manifest money. But, in fact, you can embrace this method without spending anything. For example, if you're dreaming about taking time off work to travel around the world, you could perhaps create a folder on your desktop for your future itinerary and bookmark Airbnb rentals and potential flights. Someone once said to me, rich is a state of mind, not a statement from your bank.

Writing a letter as your future self

If you could sit down a year from now and take stock of your life, what changes would you like to see? What goals would you want to have reached? What would you like to have attracted and, more importantly, what would you like to have released?

Sit and write a letter as if you already were that version of yourself, writing to the current you. Share what changes for the better have happened in your life during that year. Tell the current you how different life looks a year on, and explain what the current you will need to do, both internally and externally, to step into that future version of you.

———

The truth is, you already know subconsciously what changes you need to make for the better, and writing a letter to your future self enables you, at minimum, to acknowledge them.

Date your letter, fold it up, store it somewhere safe and then set a reminder for a year from now telling you where the letter is hidden and when to open it. An emotive way to ring in the New Year is by reading last year's letter and then sitting and writing as your future self again, ready to be opened on New Year's Eve, 365 days later.

Tip
Take a photograph of your current self to put with the letter. Notice how you can see energy shifts when you begin to look back year after year. Yes, there may be physical changes, but each picture will capture an energy shift as you embrace this more intentional, positive way of living.

Amplify your manifesting magic with... *the 369 Method*

The manifestation technique known as the 369 Method, or the Tesla 3-6-9 number theory, is named after the Serbian–American inventor Nikola Tesla. Famed for his inventions, such as the remote control and the Tesla coil, not to mention the car named after him by Elon Musk, Nikola Tesla was also known for his spiritual enlightenment. Although there is no recording of this, it was said that Tesla described the numerals 3, 6 and 9 as 'divine numbers' and felt that they held great significance in the universe, nature and the human blueprint.

When we look at numerology in the present day, the number 3 is said to be a direct link to the universe, the number 6 represents the strength we have in ourselves and the number 9 signifies the release of negative feelings – all of which are significant parts of the manifestation process.

However, it was the intuitive astrologer Karin Yee who established the now-infamous 369 Method, combining the number sequence 369 with the teachings of Abraham-Hicks, a collective of spiritual teachers channelled through speaker and author Esther Hicks. So, how exactly do you manifest using the 369 Method? Let's explore further.

The technique
Choose your manifestation

Take a pen and journal and write a single desire that you want to manifest into your life. The written desire should span two sentences on a page, taking approximately 17 seconds or more to write. Why 17 seconds? According to Hicks, it takes the brain just 17 seconds of focused concentration to begin to rewire, as we shift our thoughts to what it would feel like to receive our desire.

What could your manifestation be? This all depends on what you'd like to attract into your life. This technique has helped people welcome money, love, house moves, new jobs – the universe doesn't put a limitation on what you'd like to manifest, as long as it is safe for you, for others and for the planet.

Start the manifestation with gratitude, add in emotion and finish with the words 'into my life' – for example, 'I am so thankful for the universe aligning with me to attract my soulmate, bringing love, happiness and contentment into my life and inner peace into my heart.'

The key is to use words that amplify the emotion and energy you want to attract. As you can see here, I have used language associated with feelings such as love, happiness and contentment, which are words you can feel inside your body when reading them back.

Write your desire 3 times in the morning

For 33 days, take your journal every morning as soon as you wake up, and write your manifestation three times on the page. The key to success when manifesting anything is to focus on the feeling, on the energy of what it is you want to attract, and how it will feel when – not if – it enters your life.

Write your desire 6 times at midday

Midway through your day, take out your journal again and write the same manifestation six times. Follow the same process as before, immersing yourself in the energy of how it will feel, visualizing yourself being with your desire. Release to the universe and move on with your day.

Write your desire 9 times before bed

Finally, before bed, write the same manifestation nine times, following the same method as you used during the day. The initial three scripts were to set the intention to the universe, the following six were to amplify them, and the final nine are to set this manifestation in stone.

Tips for 369 Method success

Be sure to speak in the present, as if your manifestation is already yours. *Avoid using words such as 'I will' or 'I want', because you'd be speaking to the universe as if you do not have your desire, which leads it to deliver more of what you don't have.*

Do not obsess over your manifestation. *The how and when are not yours to consider; this is where divine timing comes into play. Trust in the universe to know that when your energy is ready to receive your desire, it will be yours.*

Trust that your manifestation could appear way before the 33 days are over! *Again, divine timing will make sure your desires appear when you are ready to accept them. If you reach the end of the 33 days and you are still waiting for magic to appear, do not give up hope. Release this into the universe and sit in the faith that it will soon be yours, because you have claimed it.*

Be consistent. *For this technique to truly work, you must set the time aside each day to write three times in the morning, six times in the middle of the day and nine times before you go to sleep. However, if for some reason you miss a day, do not fret – just jump back into the routine the very next day.*

STEP
4

Raise your vibrations

The concept of energy was introduced
on page 18, but let's now take a deeper
look at how our frequency affects our
ability to manifest.

The law of vibration

Alongside the law of attraction sits its big sister, the law of vibration. Think of the law of vibration as the jigsaw's missing piece, which many people dismiss when striving for an abundant and aligned life.

The laws of the universe are designed to be embraced together, married in harmony, to establish a life of understanding and trust.

The law of vibration states that all objects and all living things are vibrating at varying speeds, emitting different energy frequencies. The speed determines whether this is a low (slow) vibrating energy or a high (fast) vibrating energy.

The law of vibration is fundamental to manifesting because, unless we understand, how can we attune to different frequencies, it becomes almost impossible for the law of attraction to help us magnetize our desires.

If you're vibrating at a lower frequency, no amount of journaling, vision boarding and rubbing your crystals is going to increase your powers of manifestation. For example, if you want to attract more money into your life, but your thoughts are continually focused on never having enough, this 'lack' mindset will operate at a low frequency, unable to tune into the higher-frequency feelings of abundance and financial freedom. Imagine the sound of the radio when you're struggling to find your favourite station – that's how your energy is represented.

If manifesting money, for example, is a focus for you, find people, places and opportunities that make you *feel* abundant. Take your laptop to work in a fancy coffee shop for the afternoon. Look at luxury holidays online. Drive around the nicest area in town. The beauty is that abundance isn't the amount of money in your bank account – it is a feeling you can create and tune into.

There is no denying that humans are able to sense energy. Perhaps you can recall a time when you've walked into a room and sensed

> *'The beauty is that abundance isn't the amount of money in your bank account – it is a feeling you can create and tune in to'*

some form of negative energy in the air. We often refer to there being an atmosphere, but this is, in fact, your ability to tune in to a certain frequency that is being emitted.

And on the flip side of that coin, think how quickly you are magnetized to someone at a party when they vibrate at a higher rate, sitting in the energy of happiness, joy, positivity, optimism or gratitude. Because you're reading this book, I'm assuming this is the sort of energy you naturally want to gravitate toward.

In short, to consciously manifest your desires, you must understand how to move into a matching vibrational frequency first. Once you've embraced the law of vibration, the law of attraction (see pages 12–15) will enable you to magnetize those desires into your reality.

How to move into a high-vibrational state

Each living thing has its own specific vibrational frequency. It's like when you instantly click with certain people in life and not so much with others, or when you experience a really good time at a show when your friend who is standing alongside you didn't enjoy it in the slightest. This indicates that moving into a high-vibrational state is subjective and varies from person to person.

However, there are a number of tried-and-tested ways to change your energetic state. Here are 12 examples to help you experience a shift in your frequency.

Turn up the music

Music has the power to shift your soul, never mind your frequency. Think about some of the most joyful moments of your life and how music played its part: the first dance at your wedding; a party; playing music to your children. Create a playlist of your favourite songs – including songs from your happiest years – and dance around your kitchen. See how your mood shifts almost instantly after a kitchen rave.

―

Curate your feed

How often would you estimate you spend time scrolling on your phone, only to come away experiencing some form of low-vibrational state? I'm assuming for many people it is fairly frequently, because as a 30-something recovering from an addiction to her phone, I spent years doing the same.

Following Debbie Downers from school on Facebook when we didn't even exchange pleasantries in the supermarket. Doom-scrolling when there was yet another world disaster trending on Twitter. Making my way down the Instagram feed, scrutinizing myself as I went. The ironic thing is, I was choosing to spend my time absorbing this constant stream of negativity.

That was, until I chose differently. I chose to curate my feed with feel-good brands, uplifting posts and influencers with whom I resonated, rather than ones I compared myself with.

Spend time today unfollowing or muting anyone who makes you feel negative, and search for new accounts that uplift you when you scroll, rather than drag you into a downward spiral.

Add high-vibe foods to your meals

A lifestyle filled with processed, unbalanced foods, refined sugars and alcohol can seriously alter your energy vibration. By adjusting your diet to include more earth-grown foods, that are naturally balanced, vibrant in colour and nutritious, you can increase your frequency drastically – so that you glow in both the physical and the energetic sense. According to former psychotherapist Robyn Openshaw, the author of *Vibe*, there are hundreds of foods that vibrate at a high frequency, including leafy green vegetables, nuts and seeds, fresh berries, raw chocolate, herbal teas and coconut oil.

Declutter

People often underestimate how much of an effect a cluttered environment can have on the mind, forming a subtle but continuous level of stressed energy. Here is a slight twist on the KonMari Method, made famous by Japanese organizing consultant Marie Kondo. When you begin to declutter, hold each item. If it evokes negative emotion or has a less-than-desirable memory attached, throw it out, sell or return it or pass it to charity.

Switch up the flow

Transform the energy in your home by switching the room flow (but make sure the furniture is still easy to walk around). Consider implementing the ancient Chinese art of feng shui to maximize a positive energy in your living environment.

For example, according to feng shui, having your back to the door in your office signals that you are turning away from money and offers of work. To combat this, either switch your desk around or add a mirror to the wall you face, so that this energy is reflected back onto you instead of you being turned away from it.

Make time to meditate

Despite meditation having an incredible number of benefits, it can be a frustrating tool to try to grasp. Our minds are so overstimulated that even switching off for ten minutes can be hard due to the constant stream of internal chatter.

However, the art of meditation is about taking a moment to let your mind rest, rather than striving for perfection. Focus on your breathing as you close your eyes, acknowledging your thoughts as they enter your mind, and releasing them like balloons into the sky.

Meditation doesn't always need to involve sitting crossed-legged on the floor, palms up. It can also come in the shape of mindful tasks, such as creative painting, knitting or even completing a jigsaw.

Catch your negative thoughts

This is one of the first tools I used when I began the overhaul of my negative mindset – being self-aware enough to catch the thoughts before they spiralled.

Notice the negative thought and ask yourself these questions:

· Does it really matter in the grand scheme of things?

· Can you feel empathy toward that person or situation?

· Is there a silver lining in some form?

· How could you change the way you reacted?

Although this will feel unnatural at first – and it really does take work – it soon becomes second nature to override the way your mind reacts to negative situations.

Ground yourself

One of the most powerful yet easy ways to realign your frequency is to ground yourself into the earth. Take off your shoes and step on the grass outside, feeling yourself connect without barriers.

Overhaul your diary

Is your brain awash with dates, birthdays and to-do lists? Sit down and plan your month ahead, either in a physical diary or using an app. This is more strategy-based than spiritual, but the feeling of overwhelm can rapidly lower our frequency, attracting more reasons to be overwhelmed.

Shop for plants

Why not introduce some plants to your home? Studies show that indoor plants not only reduce stress and boost mood, but can also improve concentration. Maybe it's time to add some greenery to your office?

Prioritize sleep

Getting enough sleep is imperative to living in a high-vibrational state. The trouble is, sleep is low on our list of priorities because our schedules are so full. We wake early to start the day, but resist going to bed in a bid to claw back some 'me time'.

A study by the Department of Clinical and Health Psychology at Utrecht University in the Netherlands dubbed this 'bedtime procrastination', which was later changed to 'revenge bedtime procrastination'. The 2020 pandemic saw more people experiencing this, as staying up late became a way of gaining control in an uncertain environment.

Begin your journey to better sleep by winding down one hour earlier than normal for the next week – that means no screen time before bed – and see how you start to feel ahead of your usual bedtime.

Netflix and vibe

The content we consume, especially before bed, has the power to lower or increase our frequency drastically. Consider what shows you are watching as you drift off when your mind is in theta state. (Theta brain waves occur when you are drifting off to sleep, sleeping lightly and dreaming, or about to wake up. They are thought to be involved in processing information and making memories.) Do you want to reprogram with stressful, dark, scary content? If not, swap your viewing choices a couple of times a week.

———

Protect yourself from negative energies

According to the entrepreneur and motivational speaker Jim Rohn, 'You are the average of the five people you spend the most time with.' This is why evaluating your relationships every now and then can be beneficial to both personal and spiritual growth.

Just as we can tune in to other people's energy, we can absorb the energy they are emitting. For example, someone's laughter can make us laugh – it's contagious. Similarly, a colleague's bad mood has the ability to change the atmosphere of the entire office. It's soul-sucking.

———

Take a look at the friendships and relationships you have in your life at the moment. Who are your energy vampires? The focus on this chapter isn't about cutting people off who may be going through a difficult time in life. Only you know the difference between someone who is having a tough season and someone who is habitually negative. We're here to talk about navigating the latter.

Family

Coping with negative family members can be extremely challenging, especially as removing ourselves from situations isn't as simple as it might be with friends. We get to choose our friends, but we don't have the same privilege when it comes to biological family.

However, it doesn't always mean we have to distance ourselves entirely – communication and understanding can be a good starting point. We often forget, especially when it comes to parents, that they are people with real lives, past emotions and memories that may be causing their limiting beliefs to be pushed onto us. Surprise, surprise, they're not just 'the parents'.

When someone projects a negative opinion onto you, it can often be because you are mirroring something they don't like within themselves.

If open communication isn't an option, practise detachment. This can come in the form of not participating in triggering conversations, leaving the room, changing the subject or avoiding certain topics of conversation to begin with.

Friends

As sad as it may feel, some friendships aren't designed to be in our lives for ever. Some people enter our lives for a season and then leave when we transition into our next chapter. Sometimes it really is as simple as our energies aligning perfectly for a moment in time, before gently moving on.

Nevertheless, if I were to share some big-sisterly advice, I'd suggest that cutting out toxic friends has to be your first port of call. You know the friendships that empty your cup but have no intention of helping you refill it? The ones that fill your mind with limiting beliefs rather than words of support. The ones that make you feel depleted when you leave their company. This is the epitome of an unbalanced friendship, in my humble opinion.

Rather than focusing on spending less time with people you don't align with anymore, make a conscious effort to call in new friendships. This way, your time will be spent with people who lift you up, rather than on friendships that don't serve you anymore.

It really can be as simple as asking the universe to help you call in soulmate friendships, ones that amplify the mindset and vibration of life you are now embracing. You could create a vision board of how

'It really can be as simple as asking the universe to help you call in soulmate friendships'

you'd like your friendships to feel, what you'd like to do together, the freedom you'd feel when no longer fighting against the constraints of a toxic friendship.

Although it's possible, your manifestation of a soulmate friendship isn't likely to turn up knocking on your doorstep, so why not meet the universe halfway and look at places where your soulmate might spend time? Do you enjoy yoga? Then look for a local class. Do you love spirituality? Consider signing up for a course on crystal healing. Surround yourself with like-minded, high-vibe people and see how your frequency increases.

Work

One of the most frequent questions I receive with regard to vibrations is how to navigate a toxic work environment. We spend a large portion of our lives at work, so when we are in a space that affects our mental health negatively, my first answer is always to look for a way out.

———

There is a very valid fear, especially in an uncertain economic climate, that employment is hard to find. And while it might be challenging, continuing to work in a toxic workplace will only further harm your confidence and your drive – ultimately making it even harder to leave.

You have a choice.

Begin by making a plan of action, updating your resumé and signing up to notifications on job websites. Your energy will shift the moment you take back control.

If you enjoy your job but struggle with negativity from co-workers, avoid getting caught up in office gossip and politics. Yes, you can listen to other people's perspectives, but idle gossip is a drain on energy resources.

We often find ourselves standing around the metaphorical water cooler because we are programmed to feel safer in packs, rather than being the lone wolf. However, this only feeds negativity.

Make a list of all the positive aspects of your job, and focus on your gratitude for these daily. If there are certain tasks you enjoy, make these a priority and ask for more responsibility in these areas.

If you find power in crystals, black tourmaline is a great stone for warding off negative energy, so have this either on your desk or on your person.

Sometimes all that is left to do is fight negativity with kindness in a bid for the energy you emit to be absorbed by Sheila in accounts. Share good news, give people genuine compliments, listen to their stories and subtly help them to reframe their mindsets. You may be comfortable on this journey, but others are still in the depths of where you once were – kindness and compassion should come before anything else.

Where are you leaking energy?

An energy leak is a hole in your life that is leaving your reserves depleted. Like a leaking pipe in the house, plugging this is essential to halt any long-term damage.

Leaking energy can come from energy vampires, as mentioned previously, but also from feeling obliged to say yes when all you want to say is no. It can also be the result of not setting clear boundaries, avoiding difficult but needed conversations or adopting a 'why me?' mentality. Once you begin to understand and acknowledge where you are leaking energy from, you are able to begin the growth process of 'plugging', which means actively finding a solution.

Amplify your manifesting magic with… a forgiveness ritual

Holding on to resentment and anger causes huge leaks in your energy, without you consciously knowing it. When you hold any form of negative feeling toward yourself or others, you are sitting in a mindset of disempowerment.

Keeping hold of guilt, anger and shame internally will only affect you, your growth and your future. I am not saying that whoever or whatever wronged you is right – life can throw at us some truly horrific experiences that no human should have to process – but I am saying you have the choice to release this negativity causing 'dis-ease' within your body.

Forgiveness ritual

1 Begin by making a list of every single negative memory you still hold in your body. It could be someone stealing from you, it could be dealing with a bully, it could even be a time when you treated someone poorly. We assume that forgiveness is external, but the truth is, we need to forgive ourselves to see real shifts. Regardless of whether it was yesterday or 20 years ago, if you can still recall it, the emotion needs to be brought forward and released.

2 Take your list and read each sentence out loud. Following that, say the words, 'I forgive you and I release you'. As you speak this into the atmosphere, focus on the emotion and strength of forgiveness. Feel the hold that memory had on you release its grip.

3 Tear your paper into pieces or, better still, burn it in a safe environment and notice how your connection to those feelings is released along with the smouldering ashes.

4 You may feel drained the next day, as your body recovers from an emotional hangover. Stay hydrated, mentally rest and be gentle with yourself for the following 24 hours.

STEP
5

Embrace the energy of gratitude

When we consider the emotions and thoughts that increase our energy frequency to a high-vibrational state, gratitude is among the most impactful. In fact, it could be said that gratitude has even more influence over our ability to attract our desires than joy and happiness do.

Giving thanks

The truth is, sitting at a level of joy all the time isn't feasible – nor is it healthy. This is why leaning into the energy of gratitude feels easier, because regardless of your mood, there is normally something to feel thankful for.

Being in a state of happiness simply isn't possible 100 per cent of the time – nor should it be. As a soul living a human experience, we have to embrace a rainbow of emotions to truly understand how finding the pot of gold at the end feels.

Although we talk about low-vibrating emotions, there is no such thing as a 'bad' feeling. Even those emotions on the lower end of the vibrational scale need to be embraced and worked through in order to be released. However, living in a state of gratitude – having the ability to count our blessings – is something that can be adopted, even on the most challenging of days.

Take a look around you now and make a mental note of ten things you are thankful for. It can be as simple as the glass of water you have available to you, or the money that enabled you to buy this book. Perhaps it's the fridge filled with food, or the fact that your afternoon meeting has been cancelled. We love a cancelled meeting, right?

Not only does gratitude have the ability to shift our vibrations, but when we swap our grey-tinted glasses to those with a slightly more rose-coloured

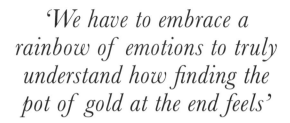

'We have to embrace a rainbow of emotions to truly understand how finding the pot of gold at the end feels'

filter, suddenly we see the world with a little more colour again. When we focus on the abundance we have in life, things don't seem as tough as they might have done to start with.

And guess what happens when we focus on the things we are thankful for in daily life? The universe delivers more things to be grateful for.

After all, the law of attraction states that like attracts like, so start to consider what you would like to receive more of, and focus on putting exactly that back out into the world.

Abundant mindset vs. lack mindset

The difference between an abundant mindset and one of lack can alter how resilient we are, how we cope with stress and even how our immune response functions. This is about far more than writing down three things you are grateful for and expecting the universe to deliver our desires.

Developing an abundant mindset allows you to live a full and satisfied life, feel creative and inspired, take advantage of new opportunities that come your way and feel more secure in who you are.

So, what is the difference between a lack mindset and an abundant one?

• A lack mindset focuses on never having enough, while an abundant one knows there's more than enough for everyone.

• A lack mindset critiques and points out errors, while an abundant one offers appreciation and searches for solutions.

• A lack mindset sees pitfalls and avoids taking any risk, while an abundant one sees opportunity and embraces change.

If you were to take an honest look at your thought pattern right now, which camp would you fall into – lack or abundant? Let me reiterate what I spoke of earlier – whatever thoughts are on repeat right now, your mind will do everything in its power to prove you correct. Like inventor Henry Ford famously said, 'Whether you believe you can do a thing or not, you are right.'

When you are in an abundant mindset, it creates a ripple effect of positive things happening around you, such as green traffic lights when you're in a rush, someone holding the train doors open for you, or receiving a voucher for a free coffee.

Contrary to that, when you are in a lack mindset, problems will occur, such as your car needing to be fixed out of the blue, or an unexpected utilities bill – which then only further reaffirms the feelings of lack.

However, I want to be careful not to associate the term 'abundant' with money. 'Abundant' has been used as a financial adjective in recent times, but to be truly abundant means to be rich in life. Rich in health. Rich in love, friendships and soulmates. Rich in opportunities. Rich in peace. Rich in clarity. Rich in alignment. Those are signs of true abundance.

It is easy to be consumed by all the things that are wrong in the world. We are fed negativity every day by the media, both online and offline – yet there are so many amazing moments happening all around us.

When you next go on a walk, I challenge you to really take in your environment and see how many things there are to be grateful for, from the leaves changing colour to the children you hear laughing in the park.

The key to flicking the switch on your mindset from lack to abundant is making it a daily focus. An authentic focus, at that.

There is no point in writing a gratitude list each day if you simply go through the motions as part of a morning routine. The magic comes when you embrace the energy of true gratitude. How can you do this? By imagining what life would be like without the things you already have.

How to foster an abundant mindset

Moments of reflection

Before bed, take some time to either mentally list, or physically make a note of, three things from your day that you are grateful for. What can often happen with spiritual self-care routines is that they become automatic, and we skip the essential part where we lean in to the energy of being truly thankful. Be sure to imagine life without those three moments of your day to help conjure the feelings of gratitude.

What if…?

The question of 'What if…?' is both a helpful and an unhelpful thinking style, which humans developed as a safety mechanism during evolution. What if the worst happens? What if it doesn't pay off? What if they don't like me? What if it doesn't turn out the way I hoped?

However, what if you turned this question on its head? What if the best outcome happened? What if it really does work out? What if it turns out even better than you imagined?

Cultivating a 'possibilities' mindset like this starts to rev the engine of your mind to look for solutions rather than problems, moving you into an abundant frame of mind, rather than one of lack.

Win-win mentality

What can often happen when we are in state of lack is that, when someone else wins in life, we assume that there is nothing left for us. But let me share how an abundant mindset might look at this.

———

When the universe shows us a win in life, that is without doubt a sign sent to showcase exactly what is possible. Not just for the person who had the win, but for you. There is power in witnessing another person's achievements, because the moment you can see it, you can start to believe it, and the universe can help you achieve it, too.

Revel in other people's celebrations just like you would your own. Rather than using your energy to feel envy or jealousy, use it to define your own version of success, work on your own metrics of life and prepare yourself for the magic the universe is about to deliver.

Cause or effect

When you have an abundant mindset, you live with a more holistic approach to problem-solving. Rather than looking externally at who or what is to blame, you reflect internally and see where the solution may lie. This is called the law of cause and effect.

———

Put in its simplest form, this law states that every action has a reaction, and every reaction has its action. Every thought we have, every word we speak, sets a chain of events in motion. For every action and reaction, there can be a positive and a negative outcome.

We can be 'in effect', where everything happens to us, it is always someone else's fault, something else was to blame. Or we can be 'at cause', where we look to see how we let something affect us, how the way we reacted could have changed our path, and how we now get to decide the way in which we will control.

An abundant mindset asks if there is a lesson or a blessing in the challenge, and if so, how it can be embraced.

Wanting more

When we start to focus on adopting a more grateful approach to life, a recurring thought can often be, 'How can I want more when I'm supposed to be happy with my lot?' It sounds counterintuitive, right?

———

And, yes, while much of fostering an abundant mindset comes with being happy in your current reality, you can absolutely still want more in life.

It is safe to have desires that move you from your current reality. It is healthy to want to better your life, achieve new goals and call in your manifestations – all while being grateful for your life at this point.

Let's take manifesting your dream house as an example. If you look at gratitude in its most basic form, to have a roof over your head is one of the most notable blessings you can have in life, alongside health, food and water. But this doesn't mean you can't desire more from your living situation.

As I was manifesting the house I had on my vision board, which had a garden and no noise from the neighbours, I still took time to appreciate the small details of my apartment that made me fall in love with it all those years ago.

I knew from the law of attraction that if I was to manifest a home that ticked the boxes on my cosmic shopping list – garden, quiet, home office, fireplace, original features, pantry in the kitchen, ample parking, street where the neighbours said good morning to one another – I'd have to create a living environment where I could access the portal of feel-good energy while I manifested the house.

I began by creating an indoor garden and nurturing each plant as it grew. I bought a fire surround from a second-hand shop and decorated it just as I would when I had a real fire burning on a cold autumn evening. I bought glass jars and became an Instagram sensation (OK, five of my friends commented) simply by tipping my flour and cereal into them and using my label maker. The row of jars was the closest thing I could get to a pantry.

And within one month, my dream house came on the market and, in the fullness of time, was signed, sealed, delivered – and all mine.

Let me reaffirm, you can still desire more, while being grateful for what you have. You can embrace the energy of peace with your current situation *and* the wish for something better.

Amplify your manifesting magic with… the boomerang effect

What we put out into the world we receive back, much like a boomerang – which is why giving is such an important part of living in an abundant state.

Generosity has the ability to shift your energy, because giving back in one form or another feeds the soul. How good does it feel when you know you've helped someone? Or when you've given back in some way and that warm feeling creeps over you?

Whether that is sharing time, money, a smile or a shoulder to cry on, if everyone did just a small bit to help someone or something they felt aligned with, we could create a powerful shift in the frequency of the world.

Giving to others is, in fact, a survival instinct. Sharing food with the hungry, and giving warm coats to those who are cold, are examples of humanity's intrinsic generosity. And by doing this, we've prolonged the survival of the human race. Imagine what would have happened to the world if we were all born thinking only of ourselves.

Here are 22 ways you can create a boomerang effect with the universe, by giving back to others.

1   Set up a regular standing order to a charity close to your heart.

2   Donate clothes.

3   Give make-up/toiletries to a women's shelter.

4   Ring a friend to listen, not talk.

5   Make someone a cup of tea.

6   Tip your barista a little more than usual.

7   Smile at a stranger.

8   Walk your neighbour's dog.

9   Donate blood.

10 Give old bedding and towels to an animal shelter.

11 Shop from a small business.

12 Publicize a friend's business on social media.

13 Join the Be My Eyes app, where you answer questions via video chat for a visually impaired person.

14 Pay someone a genuine compliment.

15 Offer your time to a local charity.

16 Leave your finished book on a bench or at the bus stop for another person to read.

17 Write a note of kindness and pin it up where someone will find it unexpectedly.

18 Donate canned food to a local food bank.

19 Buy a second lunch and give it to someone in need.

20 Plant a tree.

21 Pick up rubbish as you see it.

22 Spread happy news on social media to override the negativity.

STEP
6
Believe

We've reached the part of the manifestation
process that causes so many of us to stumble
– believing. This means believing your desires
are available to you, and that you are worthy
of receiving them.

Allowing yourself to believe

Believing in the power of manifesting isn't just about allowing your mind to potentially consider a higher source; it's also about being able to sit in the energy of believing your desires can one day be yours. Surprisingly, the latter is often the biggest struggle.

As you've got this far, I'm assuming you have a sliver of belief when it comes to universal powers, energy and the concept of shaping our reality with our thoughts. Perhaps you're starting to believe there could be some unexplainable magic at play here, and you're ready to utilize this same magic on a conscious level.

Think back to all those times when you've manifested without realizing: when you've thought about someone, and they've called, or you've imagined a scenario at work, and it's played out almost exactly as the vision you had in your mind's eye. That's the universe right there, my friend.

However, the reality is that you can be spiritually connected to a higher source and still struggle to manifest. Why? Let me introduce you to limiting beliefs.

What are limiting beliefs?

Limiting beliefs are the biggest saboteurs of manifestation, causing energy barriers that the universe just isn't able to break through. After all, if you don't believe you are worthy of having something, how can you become an energy match for it?

At the root of a limiting belief sit emotions such as shame, guilt, insecurity or even anger. These emotional reactions lead to behavioural patterns that could include self-sabotage, poor money management, not wanting to look after our bodies, or arguing with people we love.

Until the age of about seven, our subconscious mind runs the show. The subconscious has control over physical functions, like breathing, blinking and digestion. When we are young everything we receive through our senses is filtered through our subconscious as a fact.

However, when we turn seven or so, the conscious part of the mind begins to develop, helping us form our own set of opinions. We absorb beliefs from our parents, guardians and teachers, taking in views on the world, and understanding what behaviour is or isn't acceptable.

This formation of the conscious part of the brain can last right up until your late teens or early twenties, which is why, when we first start to unearth limiting beliefs, they can often stem from our childhood and teenage years.

For example, your parents or guardian might have repeatedly spoken about how they had to work incredibly hard to put food on the table, and while there's no denying their reality, you were programmed to believe that life always had to be a struggle.

Or perhaps you hold a memory of laughing loudly in the garden with friends and an argument erupting at home, which led you to believe that happy moments don't last for long, and that good times disappear as quickly as they arrive. This then stops you from fully enjoying life as you grow older.

Maybe you don't feel worthy of receiving love because of language used in an early teenage relationship.

Or perhaps you were continually compared with a sibling who was dubbed the high achiever, and now you've settled for a job you dislike, all because you've assumed you'd fail if you tried your hand at a career that lights you up.

However, just as you have formed beliefs and opinions before, the brain's neuroplasticity – its ability to adapt as a result of experience – means it has flexibility and can be rewired and reprogrammed, time and time again. Rather than having a fixed mindset and believing that nothing can change and life is just the way it is, we have the ability to create new pathways and new beliefs to help us experience life differently.

Positive thoughts create new pathways. Repetition and practice strengthen these pathways, creating new behaviours and actions. The old pathways, meanwhile, get used less and ultimately weaken.

Five ways to break limiting beliefs

For the purpose of this exercise, let's take an example of a limiting belief linked to a particular area of your life, and examine how to use each stage to break it down. The limiting belief we'll look at is: 'It is too hard to start my own business.'

Acknowledge

To discover what limiting beliefs you have, begin by writing down what comes to mind when you think about reaching your particular manifestation. Taking our example, you may want to leave your 9–5 job and build a business of your own, but you feel overwhelmed at the thought of everything you'll need to do, so you resign yourself to the thought that it's just too complicated.

Challenge yourself

Once you have observed your limiting thoughts, challenge yourself by asking the following questions:

- Is this a belief or a fact?

- Have I always thought this way?

- Can I trace back to where this belief may stem from?

- Does this belief serve me, and how is it affecting my life?

Argue for and against

The next stage is to disempower the belief by finding both supporting and opposing arguments.

It may feel counterintuitive to find supporting evidence – after all, why do you want to prove the belief right? But the reason we begin with evidence for is so we can then create arguments against each point. This allows us to question the validity of our initial limiting belief.

For example, your limiting belief that it is too hard to start your own business may have supporting evidence resembling any of the following:

1 You launched a business a number of years ago and didn't make a sale in your first week, so you closed it down.

2 You began the process of registering a new business and felt so overwhelmed and out of your depth with legalities that you instantly clicked off the website.

3 Your parents were self-employed and the language used throughout your childhood was often negative, only reaffirming what you believe to be true.

4 You don't have all the skills needed to navigate a website build, social media, marketing and everything else the internet now tells you a business needs at its inception.

Now look at the argument against each of those cases, as shown below:

1 Yes, you may have launched a business before, but was this really what you wanted to do? Perhaps it wasn't the right time in the market – or the right time in your life. Did you give it long enough?

2 You can access advice online and over the telephone to break down the procedure for registering your business. Take small steps to stop the feeling of overwhelm. Have you purchased a house before or registered for something else in life with paperwork? Think about those times as evidence that you can do it.

3 While your parents may have suffered with limiting beliefs, you are fortunate enough now to have the tools available to work through these yourself. Look at the resources your parents had available compared with what you now have. You have the chance to stop this generational belief being passed down any further.

4 You may not have the skills now, but think about a time when you started something new – perhaps a new job with unfamiliar processes and computer systems – and you learned. This is exactly what you can do with your own business: learn as you go. Websites such as YouTube enable you to become self-taught in most things, so don't let the fear of not knowing something make you think you can't learn it.

Create a new belief

Can you see how arguing the case against your limiting belief has already allowed you to reframe your thinking? Now let's look at creating a new belief. Decide how you want to feel. What are you looking for? What do you want to achieve? What thoughts will help you reach that point? For instance, the new belief we could create for the example we've been looking at might be:

'I have the power to overcome any obstacle with ease and flow, and am ready to step into the version of me who runs a successful business.'

Once you have chosen your new belief, begin to mentally rehearse the outcome you would like to experience, such as seeing sales notifications coming through on your phone, or wrapping your orders to be posted out.

Take action

Once your thoughts begin to change, your behaviour and actions will alter. Strengthen your new belief by taking the kind of action you would if your belief were a fact. For example, your new belief is that you have the ability to break through any obstacle to create a successful business, so taking action could include finally investing in website hosting. Or perhaps signing up for a course that teaches you how to make the most of your email marketing. A by-product of strengthening your belief with direct action is the evidence you are then able to store in your mind in support of it. Feeling yourself slip back into that limiting belief? Pull forward the evidence of when you researched website hosting or completed the email marketing course.

Surround yourself with expanders

When we have a limiting belief, our minds will go in search of examples to prove it's a fact. With our belief example, this 'proof' may come in the form of noticing businesses closing down, seeing friends struggling with monetizing their passion projects, or spotting news headlines reporting the challenging economic climate.

To change this limiting belief, we need to surround ourselves with expanders. These are people who are living the life you want to live, doing the things you want to do. Expanders show you what is possible, because they are people just like you.

One way to do this is to curate your social meda feed with people who are successful in the area you want to focus on. Surround yourself with the energy you want to create for yourself and see how quickly your limiting beliefs start to waver.

―――

'Expanders show you what is possible'

Amplify your manifesting magic with...
EFT tapping

Emotional Freedom Technique (EFT), or tapping as it is more commonly known, is an alternative medicine established in the mid-1990s by Gary Craig, a Stanford University engineering graduate and ordained minister. Despite being largely considered a pseudoscience by those in the medical field, this evidence-based self-help method has been cited in hundreds of studies as a proven technique to help with issues such as anxiety, post-traumatic stress disorder (PTSD) and even physical pain.

EFT focuses on tapping with your index and middle fingers on different meridian points around the body, much like those used in acupuncture, to rebalance the flow of energy. Traditional Chinese medicine sees the meridian points as pathways that allow energy to move around the body. When they become unbalanced or blocked, it is said to cause unease and possibly even sickness in the body. Stimulating these points through finger tapping, however, is an easy way to restore unsettled energy.

When we look at EFT with regard to manifestation, the aim is to change the negative energy in our pathways to a positive energy by repeating different statements to evoke particular emotions and reset our focus.

For example, we may be feeling despondent and as though nothing is going our way, but with this method we are able to move from a negative, unbalanced state to a neutral state and then to a receptive one, open to possibilities. If you wish, you can think of EFT as a video game; as you tap, you are breaking through each level until you reach the winning podium.

A beginner's guide to meridian points

Using your index finger and your middle finger together, tap on each point illustrated. It doesn't matter which side of your face you tap on or whether you use your left or right hand.

1 Side of the hand that forms a karate chop

2 Crown of the head

3 Top inner corner of the eyebrow

4 Side of the eye

5 Under the eye on the fleshy part of your cheek

6 Above your cupid's bow

7 Middle of the chin

8 On the collarbone

9 Below the armpit

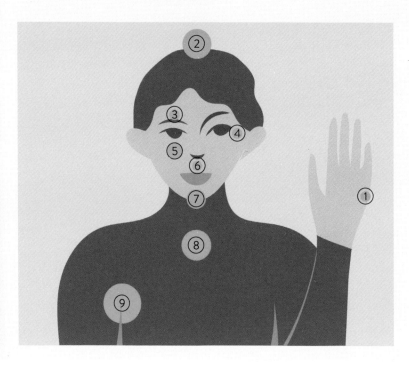

How to use EFT tapping to shift into a possibilities mindset

Begin by choosing an issue for which you want to shift the energy. Let's say the issue is, 'I feel like my manifestation will never become my reality.'

As you begin tapping, move through the meridian points, tapping on each one while repeating the following statement: 'Even though I feel like my manifestation will never become my reality, I deeply and completely love and accept myself.'

Moving through this sequence, the key point to remember is to allow yourself to experience the same emotions you have when this limiting belief rears its ugly head. Be as sad, angry and deflated as you need to be. You can only release these feelings when they are brought to the surface and acknowledged.

You then move into a neutral energy state by repeating a 'maybe' phrase, such as, 'Maybe I could choose to let go of this limiting belief and start to see things in a different light'. At the same time, again make your way through the meridian tapping points, focusing on the energy of possibility. How would you feel in a state of neutrality?

Once you feel in a more neutral state – signs of this shift may include the speed or tone of your voice changing, your posture moving or your facial expressions altering – you then begin to tap in your new positive belief: 'I am worthy of everything I desire, and I am ready to step into the person I need to be to welcome my manifestations.' Continue to be mindful of the emotions you feel; you are aiming for a heightened state of excitement, joy and positivity during this final round of balancing your meridian points.

EFT script for achieving your goals

While this is a beginner's guide to the EFT, below I have included a more in-depth, interchangeable script for you to follow and adapt once you become familiar with the meridian points across the body. This script can be customized to help shift whatever belief you may be struggling with.

Negative phase

• Karate chop meridian point: Even though I feel like I will never be able to attract my manifestations, I deeply and completely love and respect myself .

• Crown of the head meridian point: Even though I feel like I will never achieve my goals, I deeply and completely love and accept myself.

• Inner corner of the eyebrow meridian point: Even though I feel like every time I start a new habit, I fail, I deeply and completely love and accept myself.

• Side of the eye meridian point: Even though I feel like I will never be able to attract my manifestations, I deeply and completely love and respect myself.

• Under the eye meridian point: Even though I feel like I will never achieve my goals, I deeply and completely love and accept myself.

• Top of the lip meridian point: Even though I feel like every time I start a new habit, I fail, I deeply and completely love and accept myself.

• Middle of the chin meridian point: Even though I feel like I will never be able to attract my manifestations, I deeply and completely love and respect myself .

• Collarbone meridian point: Even though I feel like I will never achieve my goals, I deeply and completely love and accept myself.

• Under the arm meridian point: Even though I feel like every time I start a new habit, I fail, I deeply and completely love and accept myself.

Neutral transition phase

· Karate chop meridian point: Maybe I could start to see these beliefs differently.

· Crown of the head meridian point: Maybe I could change these beliefs.

· Inner corner of the eyebrow meridian point: Maybe I could let go of these beliefs go.

· Side of the eye meridian point: I choose to let this go.

· Under the eye meridian point: These are just stories that I have told myself.

· Top of the lip meridian point: What if I allowed myself to tell a different story?

· Middle of the chin meridian point: What if I allowed myself to see this differently?

· Collarbone meridian point: What if I allowed myself to believe something different?

· Under the arm meridian point: I choose to let go of these beliefs go and start afresh.

At this point, ask yourself whether you feel a shift in energy. If not, repeat the neutral transition phase again until you do. If so, move forward.

Positive phase

- Karate chop meridian point: I am ready to step into the person I need to be.

- Crown of the head meridian point: I achieve anything I put my mind to.

- Inner corner of the eyebrow meridian point: The universe is supporting me on my path to greater good.

- Side of the eye meridian point: People reflect who I am and what I believe – they now reflect back to me the high vibration I put out into the world.

- Under the eye meridian point: I am worthy of my desires.

- Top of the lip meridian point: I am ready to welcome a flow of abundance into my business.

- Middle of the chin meridian point: I am energetically ready to achieve my goals.

- Collarbone meridian point: I welcome more love and more connection.

- Under the arm meridian point: I am the creator of my life.

Close your eyes, put your hands on your lap, facing upward, and take a deep breath.

STEP
7

Take action

If you have dabbled with the teachings of the law of attraction before picking up this book, you may be familiar with the ideology that you can attract your greatest desires just by the thoughts you choose. Many a manifestation guru will tell you that if you ask, it shall be delivered. And, to a certain degree, this is true.

Putting action into the law of attraction

There is real power in aligning yourself with the energy you want to attract and then simply releasing your grip. This is the beauty of manifestation. You call in your desire and the universe co-creates to help make it, or something better suited, happen.

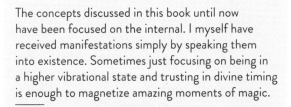

The concepts discussed in this book until now have been focused on the internal. I myself have received manifestations simply by speaking them into existence. Sometimes just focusing on being in a higher vibrational state and trusting in divine timing is enough to magnetize amazing moments of magic.

But the more positive action you take toward your manifestation, the more aligned your final results will be. This is the moment spirituality blends with strategy.

Think of that first step of inspired action as a single lightbulb, which then illuminates the whole path for you to walk down. Following that initial gut feeling activates a chain of events to guide you to your desire.

> *'This is the moment spirituality blends with strategy'*

Introducing universal downloads

While action in the traditional sense is results-led and solution-focused, inspired action is more connected to a strong inner urge to do something related to the vision of your dream life.

Imagine this action being your internal compass guiding you toward your manifestation by taking some form of step in that direction, whether it be the sudden pull to pitch an idea to your boss or saying yes to a last-minute invite.

Intuitive nudges such as these are referred to spiritually as universal downloads. The term implies that the mind is like a computer hard drive, and the universe has the power to send through ideas, signs and pointers to help steer you in the direction of your dreams.

With self-awareness and practice, over time you will begin to recognize when you receive a download from the universe. It may register as a thought, but the feeling of guidance will come from being in tune with your gut. Gut feelings are the most powerful indicators on earth, yet many people simply override or ignore theirs.

Universal downloads arrive when the volume of the outside world has been turned down. Just ten minutes of meditation a day can clear your channels sufficiently to enable the universe to connect. If you struggle with sitting in silence, consider guided meditations on YouTube or apps such as Headspace and Calm. Getting outside to walk and breathe in some fresh air is also a great way to allow universal downloads to come through. Take your phone in your pocket if you'd rather have it with you, and focus on allowing your mind to have space. In addition, downloads can come through as you sleep, in the form of vivid dreams, as you tune into your subconscious mind. Have a notebook and pen at the side of your bed so you can jot down any ideas or thoughts that come to you before you forget and start the morning.

Taking risks

Can I share a piece of advice? If you feel truly aligned with your manifestation and you receive a download from the universe that could help you make it a reality, take action before that energy disperses.

Those of us with our own businesses and passion projects can particularly relate to this. Have you ever had an idea, put it to one side and then noticed someone else pushing forth with that very same idea? The universe gave you the helpful nudge. You didn't take a step forward to claim it, so it was given to someone else. That's not to say you can't still move forward, but ideas are channelled to us in a particular time frame for a reason. Take the step.

———

Inspired action feels exciting and motivating. It can also feel scary, but scary in the same way that starting a new adventure feels: butterflies in your stomach and a mind racing with ideas. Other times, it can feel calm and knowing, like it is just right.

When it begins to feel forced and unaligned, or you start to overthink and you find yourself strangling your desire, it's time to step back and release your grip. Ask yourself

whether you are forcing this step forward because you think you have to do something to meet the universe halfway, or because it feels good to you. What is your gut telling you at this moment?

OK, so you have an idea of how you can move your life forward. But there's one issue. Fear.

Begin by asking yourself what would be the worst that could happen if you took inspired action and for some reason it didn't work out. So, you pitched an idea to your boss and they didn't gel with it. Does that mean you'll get sacked? No; and it could mean that the universe knew there was a promotion on the horizon and now you've highlighted your tenacity and drive to the person in charge of filling that spot. It could mean that you've now planted the seeds for more responsibility within your team, meaning a pay rise.

We'll talk more about redirection over rejection on pages 138–139,

*'Gut feelings
are the most powerful
indicators on earth'*

but can you see how taking inspired action doesn't have to lead to direct results straight away? Think of it as the long game, rather than instant gratification.

Taking inspired action can feel like a risk. But know that you will be safe regardless of the outcome, and if you take a wrong turning, the universe has the map to guide you back onto the right route.

Some people go through life feeling so afraid to jump and take a risk that they end up simply existing instead of living. To live involves taking risks.

The reason we don't take risks is that we are scared of what's on the other side, even though it could be so much better than what we currently have. But what exactly is going to happen if you do 'fail'? Think about that for a second. What happens if you take some form of action toward your goal and it doesn't work out as you planned? Are you fearing judgment from other people? Are you scared of rejection?

In fact, what you are fearing is your own emotions when facing these scenarios. You don't take risks because you don't want to feel shame, you don't want to feel embarrassed, you don't want to feel stupid.

But guess what? Because you now understand that it is your own

emotions you are afraid of feeling, you have the control to change them. We all have the power to change the way we feel through our thoughts.

There have been times when I've taken a risk and it hasn't paid off in the way I imagined. When I was in my twenties, I packed up all of my belongings and moved hundreds of miles away from home to the big, bright city of London. I had dreams of living in this amazing city, falling in love, making new friends, having exciting experiences and turbocharging my career. Images of London flooded my vision board. I manifested a flat and I even manifested my boss giving me a pay rise and permission to relocate.

Thank you, universe.

Was it the happy ending that I envisioned? No. I spent a year there, feeling desperately lonely, missing friends and family and realizing that, actually, I'd fallen out of love with my career. Talk about a triple whammy.

But for a long time, my ego overpowered my intuition. Intuitively, I was being guided back home, to create roots somewhere else, but my ego had other ideas.

What is the ego?

While intuition is the soul's way of guiding us onto the path of greater good, the ego is focused on survival and making sure our basic needs as living creatures are taken care of. The trouble with the ego is that most people allow it to reign as king. That certainly was essential in caveman times, but it simply isn't necessary anymore.

The ego is critical of us and of others. There is a constant need for control. It causes us to overthink, crave validation and consider what we should do, rather than what we want to do. We second-guess our decisions. Our thoughts feel limited, in contrast to the expansiveness that comes with being intuitively led.

———

When we allow the ego to be in control, our emotional state can include feelings of blame, resentment, pride, self-importance and jealousy – all of which vibrate at a lower speed, hence the feeling of physical heaviness when we experience such thoughts.

My entire existence in this new city was led by my ego. What would people think? How could I save face? What would make me look better? I want to wrap arms around that version of me and give her a bear hug.

Distinguishing between ego and intuition

There are a number of ways to differentiate between the voice of your ego and that of your intuition.

- While the tone of your intuition will be calm and based on love, your ego will be frantic, self-deprecating and negative, raising its voice to reinforce control.

- When your intuition begins to guide you, it comes with a sense of safety and knowing, while the ego will begin to make lists of why you shouldn't do something and what negative things could happen if you continued.

- The moment you ask yourself a question, your intuition leads with an answer, while moments later the ego follows, overanalysing and questioning your initial decision.

- Your intuition gives you the freedom to flow with the energy of life, while your ego pressurizes you to make black-and-white decisions.

How to work with the ego

You may be expecting me to talk about how to combat the ego and how to silence its voice. But the truth is, the ego has its purpose. It is designed to uncover threats of danger, which is why that nagging voice focuses on the negatives when you venture out of your comfort zone.

The key to finding balance is to focus on compassion and self-love. We are designed to experience the feeling of wholeness as we live this human experience, and without the ego this wouldn't be possible.

Start by acknowledging your ego through giving it a name. My ego is called Kate. Kate only wants what is best for me, but when she starts to question my decisions, I thank her for showing concern and let her know that I'm safe and I'm ready to move into a new level of comfort zone.

Kate can say some pretty hurtful things at times. This is when I disengage with those thoughts. You see, we are not our thoughts – we are the thinker of our thoughts. Negative thoughts aren't facts. Your ego isn't the truth. So I acknowledge that this is my ego talking, and I separate my connection to it.

And what happens when you focus on building a better relationship with your ego over time? Its voice becomes quieter, you become less anxious and you are able to tune in to your intuition with ease.

So, what are you going to call your ego?

'The ego has its purpose. It is designed to uncover threats of danger'

Amplify your manifesting magic with…
Connection Journaling

In this chapter, you will have discovered a number of ways to tune in to your intuition and discover how to take inspired action, but one of the most effective methods to receive from the universe is through Connection Journaling.

1 Find a quiet, comfortable spot where you won't be disturbed, and turn off notification alerts on your phone.

2 Ground yourself by breathing in through your nose for a count of four and out through your mouth for a count of four. Do this three times.

3 Once you feel your shoulders drop, begin by opening your journal and writing down what you would like clarity on. You could ask the universe to help guide you with a decision you've been struggling to make. You could ask for clarity on what direction to take next in life. Perhaps it could be as simple as asking where your focus should be this week.

4 Concentrate on your breathing and begin writing down thoughts as soon as they enter your mind, without focusing on editing or sentence structure. This is called stream of consciousness, where you let your pen flow onto the paper and channel what you are being called to channel.

5 You may receive ideas or solutions that weren't visible in the mind-fog you were experiencing prior to this, or you may even unearth limiting beliefs (see pages 101–103 to remind yourself how to work toward releasing these).

6 Once you have reached the end of your journaling session, end your connection by thanking the universe for providing the guidance or resolution you were asking for.

The truth is, we already know the answers to the questions we pose in life. But our ego and our subconscious limiting beliefs impact our ability to listen.

——

Connection Journaling is something I added to my spiritual self-care routine during 2020, when anxiety was high and my mind – like most people's at the time of trying to survive a global pandemic – had activated fight-or-flight mode. This practice enabled me to focus on what I was being guided to do to make sure I was living in a state of calm, as well as showingme where I was leaking energy and how to navigate my way through such a challenging period. It has now become a staple in my weekly routine.

'The truth is, we already know the answers to the questions we pose in life'

STEP
8

Let go of the outcome

As we draw our teachings to a close, this
penultimate chapter provides the perfect
opportunity to talk about releasing your
attachment to the outcome. Think of it like
one big squeeze of reassurance.

The universe has your back

Understanding how to connect to the powers of the universe and integrate its laws into everyday life is nothing short of life-changing.

Fully embracing the law of attraction, however, requires trust. Learning to manifest requires faith. It requires the belief in something we're unable to physically see. It requires the strength to detach from the outcome.

When I first discovered the law of attraction, the one thing I struggled with was the concept of letting go. After all, I thought we were supposed to think about our manifestation in order for it to arrive. Aren't you supposed to take inspired action? Don't you have to visualize it being yours? How do you do that if you're also meant to let go and release it to the universe? At this point in the journey to letting go, I was internally screaming.

Even though now I class myself as a master manifester, it has taken years of consciously unlearning and relearning, and of understanding how my own energy flows, to trust that what is meant to

be mine will never pass me by. And every time something has passed me by that I thought I was destined for, it was because it was clearing the way for something better.

Impatience is a trait that has become more prevalent over the last four decades as advancements in technology mean we no longer have to spend time waiting for anything. Microwaves enable us to have heated food in minutes. We can access the internet in the palms of our hands. We can get delivery of our online order within just 24 hours, sometimes even sooner. It's no wonder we ask the universe for our manifestation and then five minutes later pace around the room, wondering if it's somehow got lost en route.

Only through my journey with learning how to consciously manifest have I been able to experience the power in surrendering the how and when.

You see, when it comes to manifestation, we can work on our

internal beliefs, we can connect to the universe and call in our desires, but how and when they arrive at our front doors isn't something we can control. And neither should it be. Life is about co-creation.

When you call in your manifestation and then continue to ask, wonder, check, change your mind and check again, you slowly but surely strangle your desire. You may as well call up the universe and explain there is no trust.

Imagine going into a restaurant, placing an order and then standing behind the chef, asking when it's going to be ready, how it's going to be served and what plate it will arrive on. Can you imagine?!

Holding your desires in such a tight grip is what we call being a controlling manifester. When you're in this control stage, you can feel a real shift in your vibration, moving closer to desperation and further from alignment.

Over the years, I've received hundreds of emails from manifesting beginners, explaining how they've written a letter of gratitude to the universe, they've changed their mindset, they've

been putting goodness out into the world – and now they want to know what else they can do to speed up the arrival of their manifestation.

My reply is always this. At the heart of manifestation lies the energy we put out, alongside the energy we receive back. What kind of energy do you think is being put out into the universe when you are doing every manifestation technique available? It indicates that you don't believe it to be yours – am I right? It suggests that you don't have trust in the universe to deliver with divine timing. That you are struggling to believe that your thoughts could ever create your reality. It is the biggest tell-tale sign of a lack mindset.

When we look for examples of detachment working, we turn to tales of people finding love the second they give up looking, or people who think they'll never find their dream home and something coming along just as they stop the search.

How do you let go of the outcome?

The honest answer to this question is that you have to be OK with your life if your manifestation doesn't come to fruition. You have to be happy with Plan B. It's about creating a life with which is so content that whatever comes your way is a blessing and a bonus.Of course, it can be hard when you are emotionally linked to a manifestation. This is especially true with manifesting a child, a relationship or a positive change in health. It is not as easy to focus on your Plan B, but it is possible. Being at peace with your life path regardless of what happens is the ultimate freedom a human can experience. Because the second you release your grip and sit in the happiness of a different outcome, the universe will deliver exactly what it is you were searching for.

Manifestation is about co-creating your life with the universe, which is why we have to trust that the universe will play its part. The universe is always communicating with you in some way, whether through signs, downloads or divine intervention. Recognizing it comes down to opening your eyes, mind and soul in order to be able to receive this communication (more on this on pages 150–153).

It may also be worth asking yourself whether you are holding on to your manifestation so tightly because of the happiness you assume it will bring when it arrives.

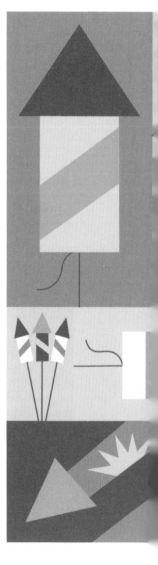

As humans, we often live in a state of recalling the past, or worrying about and planning for the future, without really embracing the fact that this very second is the only thing we can control. It is the only time we are actually present in 'being'.

We try to manifest certain things because we assume there is a level of happiness attached to them, but when we live in this mindset, rather than being happy at our core with who we are, no amount of magic from the universe will fulfil us.

We are programmed to believe that once we sign for that brand-new car, we'll feel amazing, or once our boss has agreed to a pay rise, life at work will become easier. Yes, to some extent, happiness can come from material things. But that rush of happiness comes from a fleeting release of serotonin in the brain, and then it is back to our vision boards to see what's next.

The happiness you seek now is already inside you. You don't have to wait to feel happy. You don't have to wait until you reach a certain amount in your bank account, or a particular weight on the scales or a high-up rung on the career ladder.

You are able to access the vibration of happiness simply by activating your thoughts. This is why we focused so heavily on soul goals at the beginning of this book.

Journal prompts for letting go

Here are some journal prompts to help guide you if letting go of your manifestation is something you struggle with:

• What is holding you back from fully releasing?

• What are you scared of happening if your manifestation doesn't come to fruition right away?

• What can bring you happiness and bring a calmness to your energy right now?

• While you release your Plan A to the universe to work on, what is your Plan B?

'The happiness you seek now is already within you'

How quantum shifting supports detachment

Quantum shifting, or quantum jumping, is the concept of moving into a different version of yourself in an alternate reality by choosing to live a different experience. While it may seem easy to dismiss as something you'd expect from a science-fiction film, let me explain how you've probably already quantum shifted and not realized. Remember when you were young and you hurt yourself – how quickly did the pain go away once your mother kissed it better? Or maybe your grandfather had a special concoction of hot lemonade that cured every illness and made you feel better after just one sip. The placebo effect, which is at play in these situations, is a prime example of quantum shifting.

We envision a desired state of being and we shift into that reality. The other reality is, we sit in pain and waste time when we could be playing outside with our friends. Can you see how there are different options

available to us at each moment, and how quantum shifting allows us to move into the reality most beneficial to us at that point?

There is a plethora of guided meditations available online designed to help you quantum shift. However, one of the simplest forms of jumping to an alternate reality is to imagine the version of you that has already received your manifestation. Imagine how you stand, how you talk, how you dress, how you feel – and within your mind's eye, step into that body with that new reality. Declare with confidence that you are that person.

You calmly move into the version of you that is attuned to your desires, and suddenly there is no strangling your call to the universe. There is no need to wonder about the how and when, because you have jumped into a reality where you choose a steady, non-wavering vibration. You have moved into the confident version of you that knows, without doubt, that your desires are being delivered. They are already yours and you are simply awaiting their arrival. Declare this unwavering version of yourself every day until you experience a shift in your reality.

No means next opportunity

One of the most powerful reframes you can embrace is 'no means next opportunity'. There have been times when I have felt so close to my manifestation, and then suddenly it has been snapped away. Like the time I was applying for what I was sure was my dream job as a fashion assistant for a huge magazine, but didn't get the interview. At the time, it felt like utter rejection, but just a few months later I was offered the role of assistant editor at a publishing company closer to home. While I thought I was ready to sit in the fashion cupboard assisting others, the universe had other ideas and took me closer to the top of the career ladder I was climbing at the time.

From job opportunities that I've applied for where they've picked a more suitable candidate, to relationships that haven't worked out, houses that have been snapped up by someone else, or cancelled plans, each and every time that I've taken a detour, it has been because something else is around the corner.

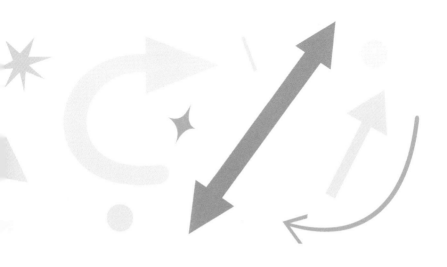

It was never rejection, only redirection.

I have had numerous conversations with people who have been trying to buy what they thought was their dream house, only to be outbid and lose it at the final hurdle. They have then gone on to find an even better house more suited to their needs, months down the line.

When you are being redirected, consider everything the universe can see that you can't.

Maybe the job you didn't get had a high level of stress attached to it. Or perhaps a relationship didn't work out because the universe already knew you weren't an energetic match. Maybe that trip was cancelled because you were being guided elsewhere in the world.

The universe doesn't want you to fail. It doesn't want to trip you up. It is there to guide you and help you in creating a life you truly love. It wants you to live the life of least resistance. This is why following your intuition, and understanding that 'no' is simply a helping hand back onto the right path, is fundamental to living a soul-centred life.

Amplify your manifesting magic with … affirmations

When we think about affirmations, the first thought that comes to mind for many is standing awkwardly in front of the bathroom mirror, pointing a finger at our reflections and telling ourselves how amazing we are. And while you may roll your eyes at the thought of repeating positive statements each day, there is real theory behind this exercise.

Simply put, words of affirmation are designed to help challenge negative thinking. The idea is to replace an old, unhelpful narrative with a more positive script in your subconscious. Each time you recite positive statements, your subconscious is being reprogrammed, because it is unable to differentiate between what is a fact and what is a belief.

You could use positive statements to boost your self-esteem, perhaps change the way you feel about your skills at work or even help with your confidence on a first date.

Regardless of whether you choose to write your affirmations each morning or repeat them out loud throughout the day, the language you choose should be realistic.

For example, if you are focusing on self-love and body image, the affirmation 'I love how my body looks in the mirror' may not resonate with you. However, changing it to 'I appreciate my body for everything it has helped me achieve so far' might be easier to believe and so embrace its energy.

As you recite each affirmation, lean in to that specific emotion. If your affirmation is 'I am confident', think about a time when you felt a level of confidence, and anchor yourself in that feeling. If your affirmation is 'I am loved', think about a time when you felt loved and appreciated by another person.

'Words of affirmation are designed to challenge negative thinking'

Throughout any manifestation practice, including affirmations, you should use the present tense – 'I am'. If you use 'I want…' or 'I will…', you are indicating to the universe that you do not have what it is you desire yet, that you are still searching for it and that you are in a lack mindset.

And just like that, we receive more opportunities to wait.

The law of attraction states that whatever we can imagine in our mind is available to be magnetized to us. By using the present tense, we are reaffirming that we already have what we desire; it is simply a case of creating the most free-flowing channel for it to be delivered through manifestation.

Bearing that in mind, here are 22 affirmations for you to pick and choose from each day. Start your affirmation journey with three to five positive statements that you feel aligned to. Change the language if needed to reflect your personal reality. Either say them out loud or write them in a notebook, being sure to evoke a positive emotion each time.

Affirmations to kickstart your day

- I accept myself unconditionally.
- I am aligned with the energy of abundance.
- I love and approve of myself.
- Following my intuition and my heart keeps me safe.
- I make the right choices every time.
- Being authentically me is my superpower and I am ready to step into this energy.

- I can do absolutely anything I put my mind to.
- The more I give, the more I will receive.
- My confidence knows no limits.
- I am a magnet for money.

- Money comes to me in expected and unexpected ways.

- I move effortlessly into abundant thinking.

- Opportunities come to me easily and effortlessly.

- I see the perfection in all my flaws.

- I have the power to create change.

- I fully approve of who I am.

- I am allowed to take up space.

- I choose peace.

- I forgive myself.

- I am excited about the possibilities of today.

- I have so much to be grateful for.

- I am worthy of having great relationships.

STEP
9

Pay attention to synchronicities and signs

From years of experience teaching the concept of manifestation, I know that experiencing synchronicities and signs from the universe is where many people truly begin their spiritual journey, moving from the evidence-based theories into accepting that there may just be something more magical at work.

Deepening your connection

As we move through life, from time to time we will be pulled toward asking the universe for guidance, especially when our intuition and ego are battling for first place as we search for clarity.

While signs and synchronicities can often be dismissed as purely coincidence, if the law of oneness is correct and everything on earth is interconnected in some form, then maybe we really are being guided by a higher source along the way. Perhaps there really is something else at play, helping steer us down paths better suited and offering us reassurance that we are on the right track.

'A setback isn't always a negative; it may be the universe's way of saving you'

What is a synchronicity?

Synchronicity is a moment with so much significance to your own reality that it is hard to ignore. Coined by the psychiatrist Carl Jung, the term synchronicity describes circumstances that appear meaningfully related yet lack a causal connection.

For example, it may be a chance meeting with someone you had thought about reaching out to, or hearing strangers talk about the very thing you are manifesting. Perhaps your book falls open to a page with a message you needed to read in that moment, or you find yourself lost on a car journey but suddenly come across a place you've always wanted to visit.

Can you see how synchronicities can feel like unexplainable but perfectly aligned moments in time? One example of a synchronicity that was so improbable that it is hard to imagine it was just random chance is the time I began speaking to a friend of mine about a retired sportsman and I decided to google where his career had taken him. The very next day, I was involved in a car crash and the same person I had been discussing the night before pulled over to check if I was OK. I find it hard to believe that the world is full of simple coincidences when something of this magnitude takes place.

How is a sign different?

A sign is when the universe responds to your direct request for support and guidance. Perhaps you ask to see something specific, like a white feather or a butterfly, to help reassure you that you've made the right decision. By connecting to the universe in this way, you open a direct channel of communication.

Five ways the universe communicates with us

Repeating numbers: Seeing repeating number sequences and patterns can indicate the universe is trying to communicate with you. These may come in the form of numbers on, for example, a receipt, a petrol pump, or even a car licence plate. There are many meanings behind each number sequence, so be sure to take note of what you are seeing and research its meaning online. Often, when I most need reassurance, I will see 11.11. For two months prior to being offered the opportunity to write this book, every time I looked at the clock or my phone, the time would be in a repeating sequence of 12.12, 14.14, 17.17, etc. And, without knowing what was in store, I knew on a soul level that this was the universe's way of saying that something amazing was around the corner.

Living creatures: Despite being interpreted slightly differently by each Native American tribe, the butterfly is thought by them to symbolize change, transformation and hope. The dragonfly, meanwhile, can indicate the need

for adaptability in life. Seeing peacocks can signify growth in your career and can hint that positive changes in this area are awaiting you.

Feathers: Feathers, and in particular white feathers, are said to be signs from the angels that you are being protected and supported on your path.

Song lyrics: When you feel a strong connection to song lyrics, explore this further as there may be a message from the universe to unearth.

Setbacks: Perhaps your flight is delayed, or you are stuck in traffic ahead of an important meeting. Maybe you've suddenly become sick before a job interview, or your date has been cancelled at the last minute. A setback isn't always a negative; it may be the universe's way of saving you – sometimes a the very literal sense. Ask yourself if you are feeling low in energy and whether these setbacks are being attracted to you by your current frequency. This may be your sign to reset.

How to ask for a sign

Sometimes your inner compass can attempt to guide you in the right direction, but the distractions of every day stop you from being able to fully see where the next turn is, or even know if you're on the right track in the first place. This is where you open your dialogue with the universe.

Start by being clear on what sign you'd like to see. Request something that you don't see every day. For example, steer clear of asking to see a pink flower if you have a garden overflowing with pink roses or hydrangeas. Perhaps your sign could be a blue gorilla or a yellow balloon. Pick something that intuitively feels aligned. It doesn't matter at this point if you can't imagine how you'd see it, because if you recall, the how and when are none of our business. The beauty of asking for something unusual is that it feels even more miraculous when it comes into your eyeline.

The next step is to verbally ask the universe for your chosen sign: 'Universe, please show me a yellow balloon to let me know I am on the right path.'

Now you release any form of control, embrace the idea of co-creating with the universe and turn your focus toward feeling good, rather than endlessly searching for anything resembling a yellow balloon. Your sign can come in a number of representations. Perhaps you'll literally see a yellow balloon floating across the sky right in front of you. But you might also see a yellow balloon on a child's sweater, or an image of a yellow balloon in a newspaper.

The first time you receive your sign, it can feel like a miracle has taken place, much like when you receive your manifestation. But this is truly the way of life that is available once you surrender to the laws of the universe.

However, what happens if you think your sign has arrived, but you are unclear as to whether it is meant for you? Perhaps you see an orange balloon instead of a yellow one and start to question whether the shade could be more mustard than orange.

The universe will deliver exactly what you have asked for in some formation, so if you find yourself in the position of questioning your sign, or feeling unclear about what it means, go back to the spiritual drawing board.

Even though it may sometimes feel easier to manipulate an unclear sign to suit your needs, this isn't a healthy way to strengthen your relationship with the universe. If you have asked for a yellow balloon, a yellow balloon it will be.

But what if your sign doesn't appear?

By now, you may have realized that patience is key to working in harmony with the higher source, but if you are still waiting for your sign to appear, perhaps this is a sign in itself.

Tune in to how you are feeling at this moment, and be guided by your gut as to where you need to turn next.

The universe is continually leading you to uncover the highest version of yourself and is there to support you unconditionally – which is why no sign could be the very sign you needed.

Signs are not your crutch

When you initially open the channels of communication with the universe, it becomes very easy to get swept up in the excitement of what is and what isn't a sign. Google becomes your best friend, and every decision you make relies on what the universe feels is best for you.

However, my advice is to not lean on signs as your crutch. Don't become dependent on asking whether everything is a sign. Sometimes in life, stuff just happens.

You will know intuitively whether or not the sign you see is aligned for you. If it is, begin to tune in to what is being channelled. There is a difference between the universe guiding you and confirmation bias, which is when your mind searches for and interprets information to support your beliefs. It is your job to understand whether you are forcing a sign or being fluid enough to receive whatever message is meant for you.

Final thoughts

When I began writing this book, my aim was to share tales of manifestation and magic I had come to experience over the last seven years. However, along the journey of putting pen to paper, I felt myself being called back time and again to discuss not only spirituality and soul, but strategy and science as well.

And when we strip away all the advice, tips and tricks, there lies the beauty of modern manifestation: that we can implement the theory behind our thoughts, behaviours and actions, but also embrace the wonderfully unexplainable magic the universe provides.

They are not separate from one another; they work in tandem, complementing each other perfectly.

In fact, to live in true harmony, one cannot function without the other. While we were initially led to believe by law of attraction gurus that all we needed to do to was think positive thoughts and watch those thoughts turn to reality, we have come to realize that, to live a life of ultimate co-creation with the universe, a few more ingredients are required.

For example, it becomes harder to reach our soul goals if we're unfamiliar with how to set intentions along the way.

It also becomes harder to take inspired action without recognizing what voice is our intuition, and what is our ego.

And that's not to mention how hard it feels to change our vibrational frequency if we don't have the knowledge of how to break through limiting beliefs.

Every page of this book is intrinsically connected to the last, forming a chain of guidance, reassurance and support, designed to be read fully and then dipped in and out of when needed.

Ironically, making a positive change often feels harder than staying in a negative bubble, but even taking the smallest tips from this book and applying them to your life will make an incredible difference.

The most important thing to note in all of this is your relationship with the universe. Manifestation isn't about asking for your desires and then expecting them to be delivered instantly. It isn't about taking and never giving back. It isn't about getting everything you've ever wished for, without, at least sometimes, meeting the universe halfway.

Manifestation doesn't always happen straight away. Sometimes we don't get what we've asked for. Sometimes we have to wait. Sometimes we have to accept that this isn't the path for us, or that we're not aligned with what we want to attract just yet.

We can't change someone's feelings toward us. We can't alter someone else's life path. We can't manipulate something for our benefit to the detriment of someone else.

But despite all of this, there is an indescribable level of excitement and hope in being divinely guided to your highest self. Every day provides new possibilities. Every twist and turn, every lesson, every blessing is part of nurturing your relationship with the universe and, more importantly, with yourself.

The feeling that comes with understanding that you are the creator of your life, that you have control over your thoughts and that you can shift your reality at any time is the epitome of freedom.

I hope throughout our journey together that you have begun to notice shifts in your life, as you focus on reframing your mindset and attuning your frequency. What starts as small shifts can soon equate to huge, life-changing moments, and before you know it, being a magnet for your desires becomes second nature.

I want you to know that you are capable of manifesting everything you desire and you are *worthy* of manifesting everything you desire. And now that you have all the tools, tips and techniques to do just that, I will leave you with one final question...

What are you waiting for?

Bibliography

Byrne, Rhonda, *The Secret*, Hillsboro, Oregon: Beyond Words Publishing, 2006.

Hay, Louise, Y*ou Can Heal Your Life*, Carlsbad, California: Hay House, 1984.

Hill, Napoleon, *Think and Grow Rich*, Meriden, Connecticut: The Ralston Society, 1937.

Kroese Floor, M., De Ridder, Denise T.D., Evers, Catherine., Adriaanse, Marieke. A. 'Bedtime procrastination: introducing a new area of procrastination', Frontiers in *Psychology*, 19 June 2014, http://www.frontiersin.org/articles/10.3389/fpsyg.2014.00611/full, (accessed August 2021).

Openshaw, Robyn, *Vibe*, New York: Gallery Books, 2017.

Peale, Norman Vincent, *The Power of Positive Thinking*, New York: Prentice Hall, 1952

Swart, Tara, *The Source: Open Your Mind. Change Your Life*, London: Vermilion, 2019.

Index

Acknowledgments

With so many amazing people in my life, where do I begin? To my family: for always believing in my dream of one day becoming a published author, for telling me a 'Jackson can do anything,' and for celebrating every success, big or small.

To my friends: thank you being that effortless support system one can only dream of. Whether we see each other daily or twice a year, I feel incredibly lucky that my biggest problem is having too many wonderful friends to mention in just this short space on a page – I could write another book on the blessings you bring into my life. I hope you're reading this knowing I mean you.

Dawn, I'm so lucky to have had you in my life for 30-something years of friendship, cheering me on, lifting me up and sharing a love of creating, dancing to 1990s R&B and bad haircuts.

Kimberly, thank you for holding me accountable during every day I put pen to paper and keeping me to a strict schedule with love. Tabara, thank you for all your guidance and belief, from one author to another. As you shared your publishing secret with me, I couldn't wait to do the same with you.

Thank you to the team at Octopus Publishing – Natalie, Sarah, Juliette, Emily, Elise and Rosamund – for giving me the chance to share manifestation with the world when I thought for so long no one would want to listen.

The Manifestation Collective community; none of this would be possible without you, from our small Facebook group of twenty in 2019 chatting all things woo-woo, to inspiring me unknowingly with your questions and quest for guidance as I wrote this book behind the scenes. Thank you for being alongside me on this journey.

Most importantly, to the universe: thank you for co-creating this amazing moment in my life. You guided me throughout, even when I thought I had no words left.

Finally, I want to dedicate this book to my darling Matilda, for making me believe I can become anything in life. Even if that anything is a glitter-covered, unicorn-loving mermaid…